Praise for **NEIL ZURCHER** and **ONE TANK TRIPS**

"Neil Zurcher's One Tank Trips have fascinated Northern Ohioans for generations . . . [This] book is loaded to the brim with some of his most memorable excursions." — *The Morning Journal*

"Sometimes humorous, sometimes touching, [Zurcher's] Channel 8 segments have made him something like Northeast Ohio's answer to the late Charles Kuralt." — *The Plain Dealer*

"While an Ohio travel book is nothing new, Zurcher's everyman approach to traveling is what sets it apart from the rest. . . . [He's] Ohio's foremost expert on off-beat attractions." — *Star Beacon*

"Zurcher writes as he speaks. Reading him, it's easy to think about jumping in the car with him to sample some new roadhouse and listening to his stories along the way." — *Cleveland Enterprise*

"Famous for his 20-year run as WJW TV 8's travel reporter, Zurcher is known for locating little-known, interesting, and unusual destinations within a day's drive of the Greater Cleveland area." – *Stow Sentry*

"Keep a copy in your boat, your car, whatever you happen to drive. . . . Neil Zurcher is a very talented writer." — *WERE AM Radio*

"The definitive guide for Ohio travelers." — *Chesterland News*

"If a cross-country odyssey to the Gulf Coast or Rockies isn't within your budget, Neil offers hundreds of closer-to-home destinations." — *Hudson Hub Times*

"If you can get there on a tank [of gas], Neil Zurcher has been there." — *Canton Repository*

"The variety of places Zurcher has found makes you wonder why you would ever have to vacation outside of Ohio . . . Enough to provide Ohioans with [a] most comprehensive, practical and entertaining travel guide." — *West Life*

Also by Neil Zurcher:

Ohio Oddities
Strange Tales from Ohio
Tales from the Road

The Best of ONE TANK TRIPS

with Neil Zurcher

Great Getaway Ideas
In and Around Ohio

GRAY & COMPANY, PUBLISHERS
CLEVELAND

This book is dedicated to:

My wife, Bonnie Zurcher;

My children: Melody Zurcher McCallister and her husband, Dr. Ernest McCallister; Melissa Zurcher Luttmann and her husband, Peter Luttmann; Craig W. Zurcher;

My grandchildren: Allison McCallister, Bryan McCallister, Ryan Luttmann, Jason Luttmann;

My parents, who taught me to love Ohio, Oscar F. Zurcher (1908–1990) and Grace Currier Zurcher (1910–1961)

Gray & Company, Publishers
www.grayco.com

This guide was prepared on the basis of the author's best knowledge at the time of publication. However, because of constantly changing conditions beyond his control, the author disclaims any responsibility for the accuracy and completeness of the information in this guide. Users of this guide are cautioned not to place undue reliance upon the validity of the information contained herein and to use this guide at their own risk.

ISBN 978-1-938441-86-8

Printed in the United States of America

2

Contents

NORTHWEST OHIO

SOUTHWEST OHIO

While We Fill the Tank

Perhaps the most frequent question I am asked is: "What's your favorite One Tank Trip?"

This book is my answer to that question because I don't have one favorite; I have many.

It's not a definitive Ohio travel book. It's a personal one, a collection of the best travel destinations I've covered in my long career as a travel reporter.

My involvement with One Tank Trips started more than 35 years ago on Fox 8 TV in Cleveland. It was just supposed to be a one-week series, but it turned into an adventure that has stretched over almost four decades of my life. And it hasn't only been on television. I also wrote on a regular basis about my travels in the AAA's *Ohio Motorist* magazine and for *The Plain Dealer*.

What I found in those years was both an education and a revelation. The revelation was the sheer number of places that I think match or supersede some of the most interesting and beautiful spots in the entire world. The most amazing part is that they are right here, a short drive from home.

To be sure, we have some major tourist attractions in the state and surrounding areas. I think most people have heard of King's Island, Cedar Point, the massive Kalahari Resort near Sandusky and other year-round water parks. Our professional and college sports teams and arenas draw lots of visitors. Our major museums and zoos are nationally known. I have visited all of these places over the years, and while I do not mean to ignore them in this book, I'm more interested in telling you about other, equally fun and interesting places that you might not yet know about.

I am in love with Ohio and the Great Lakes region. The hills, valleys, and pastures, the lakes and rivers. The cultures. The cities, villages, and even unnamed crossroads communities where time seems to stand still.

From clouds drifting in lazy mounds over Lake Erie to a fog-shrouded Ohio River where ghostly river boats, horns bellowing, glide in and out of the mist. The image of water dancing like diamonds from a waterfall in the Hocking Hills. The roar of a Saturday football crowd in a stadium. The monotonous clip-clop of Amish horses on a paved country road. The silence of a forest, broken by the scolding of a squirrel. The whisper-soft blackness of an Ohio evening punctuated by the moon and a carpet of stars that stretches to infinity.

There are also the smells. In spring, the fragrances of freshly cut grass, newly turned earth and early flowers that turn to the hot, sweet, lush smells of summer. Then the leafy wood smoke in the cool of an autumn evening that seemingly overnight slips into the white silence of a bitterly cold Ohio winter, completing the cycle and leaving the world smelling cold, fresh and new again.

These are the sights, sounds and smells of where we live, where we work and where we play.

I have gone back through scripts, stories, clippings, and video and audio tapes covering almost 40 years, and have searched out and revisited the places that I most enjoyed in my travels.

As the years went by, the way in which we wrote about trip destinations changed. Sometimes a trip meant we stopped at several places in the same area. But just as often, we highlighted only one or two attractions. What you will find in this book are the special attractions that still stand out, destinations that I fondly remember for a variety of reasons. Perhaps it was the season, a memorable meal, a place that had a special meaning to me— or maybe it was just plain fun.

These are the best of One Tank Trips, the ones I want to share with you because I enjoyed them the most. I hope you will, too.

Happy travels,

Neil Zurcher

Be Sure to Check the Location

I wrote this essay many years ago for my first travel book. It's still true today, even though nearly every car and cell phone is equipped with electronic navigation, and it deserves repeating.

There is a very good reason why the U.S. Postal Service came up with ZIP codes for our mailing addresses: They had to deliver mail in Ohio.

My wife, Bonnie, who keeps track and cares about such things as where I have been, points to the problem the postal service must have had delivering mail to Ohioans before the ZIP code era.

There are 296 towns and villages in Ohio that share the same name with another town or village in another county.

And if that is not bad enough, there are 38 instances in Ohio where three towns share the same name. Pity the poor postman who had to determine whether a letter bound for Berlin, Ohio, was meant to go to the Berlin down in Williams County, the Berlin up near Sandusky in Erie County, or the Berlin down in Holmes County where all the Amish live.

Some towns' names were so popular that they just multiplied like rabbits all over Ohio. For instance, take Avondale. There's Avondale down near the Ohio River in Belmont County, and there's Avondale over near Bellefontaine. There's Avondale near Canton in Stark County, and let's not forget the Avondale near Dayton, as well as another in Muskingum County, and the one near Cincinnati. Altogether there are six Avondales in Ohio.

And it gets worse. There are eight counties in Ohio with towns named Centerville. Now, they are probably all near the center of something, which probably accounts for the name, but it makes me wonder: Didn't anyone in town check with the post office to see whether there was another Centerville before they started painting signs at the corporate limits?

That brings us to Stringtown, Ohio, probably one of the stranger names. I can only speculate about how the name originated. Perhaps the pioneers laid out the town with bits of string to show where the various lots were. Who knows? In any event, there must have been a lot of string laid out in Ohio because Bonnie has discovered a total of 10 towns in Ohio that share the name of Stringtown.

And the postman's real nightmare was the town Five Points. The name probably originated from the early Native American trails that intersected and became roads and places of settlement. No fewer than 11 towns, villages and hamlets in Ohio bear the name Five Points.

What I am leading up to here is the importance of checking addresses and directions before starting out on a One Tank Trip anywhere in Ohio, unless you like to find yourself in unexpected places and meet people who haven't the foggiest idea what you're looking for.

For example, say you're heading to Boston to visit the Blossom Music Center. Make sure you're in Summit County. If you end up instead in Boston down in Jefferson County, you'll probably get directions to someone's orchard if you ask a local how to get to Blossom.

Even if you're a seasoned Ohio traveler and think you know where everything is in the state, you may find yourself, like I did once, in the wrong Georgetown late at night, looking for a motel that doesn't exist in the Georgetown you are presently visiting. It is only then that you discover there are six Georgetowns in Ohio, and the one that you want is at the other end of the state. At times like these, you begin to develop a real affection for the postal service's ZIP codes and curse anyone who fails to include a ZIP code in their address.

The bottom line: use your phone. Call ahead. Get up-to-date directions; ask them to send you maps or even GPS coordinates. I don't care whether you are using my travel book or someone else's, all things change with time, and if you are going to invest your family's time and money in a One Tank Trip, before you go, take a moment to confirm times, places, costs, and, especially, just which Five Corners it's in.

Using This Book

When I travel Ohio, I don't think of it broken into five exact sections: northeast, northwest, southeast, southwest, and central. Rather, I loosely imagine it as a fan spreading out from Cleveland. But to organize this book it was necessary to define some geographic areas. These groupings are meant to give a general idea of where the attractions are located, to make them easier to find on a map. This may mean, for example, that the town of Millersburg, in Holmes County, is listed in a grouping of trips in Central Ohio, while Berlin, which is Millersburg's next-door neighbor, is listed under Southeast Ohio. But don't be afraid to mix and match some of the trips that are located in adjoining geographical areas.

The destinations listed in this book have been chosen by me on the basis of my own experience and from letters and phone calls I have received from "One Tank Trips" viewers over the years. None of the destinations has paid a fee to be included in this book.

Lastly, this is not intended to be a technical reference work. You won't find maps or detailed directions. Instead, this book is meant to encourage you to get out and sample some new places that might be fun, intriguing, and, hopefully, educational. Remember, half the fun of traveling is discovery. So, get out your map and plan your trip.

I offer one bit of advice. When my wife and I are on our own One Tank Trip, and I suddenly find myself at the end of a dead-end road that wasn't on the map, and she says, "You're lost, aren't you?" I always reply, "I am not lost. I just don't know exactly where I am at this moment."

ALL OVER OHIO

Canals of Ohio

Canal Fulton, Coshocton, Grand Rapids, Piqua, Valley View

Often, when I am on a One Tank Trip and tied up in a traffic jam on an interstate highway, I daydream about what it must have been like traveling in Ohio in the past, when we didn't have limited-access highways. When life was much slower and simpler.

Long before there were interstate highways crisscrossing the Buckeye State, there were, among others, the Lincoln Highway, the National Road and U.S. Route 20.

But long ago, when Ohio first became a state at the start of the nineteenth century, much of the land was still wilderness, with only a few primitive roads. The only trails were paths once trodden by Native Americans and bison, many of them narrow, dangerous and nearly impassable to wagons.

It was in that time that our pioneer ancestors came up with a unique idea: a series of ditches, or canals that would provide a water highway from Lake Erie on the north to the Ohio River on the south.

Starting in 1825, thousands of workers using shovels and horse-drawn, earth moving equipment took seven long years to dig the ditch 40 feet wide and four feet deep for the entire 308-mile route of the Ohio and Erie Canal.

A series of locks were also built to move the canals up and over hills. Viaducts were constructed to allow the ditch to pass over rivers and streams. Reservoirs and lakes were created along the way to supply the canals with water.

The big ditch opened Ohio to the prosperous eastern markets and allowed farmers and factories in the new state to sell their products in a much wider marketplace. Now they could send and receive goods from ports on both the Ohio River and Lake Erie. Canal boats loaded with all kinds of freight moved up and down the state around the clock.

It was slow, only as fast as a man and horse or mule could walk, towing the big boats from towpaths along the edge of the canals. The journey was slowed even more by laborious maneuvering through the numerous locks along the way.

Many immigrants were on board these canal boats heading to new homes in Ohio. It was such a success that by 1855, the canal system in Ohio stretched for more than 1,000 miles of main line canals, locks, feeder canals and lakes. The streams passed through 44 of Ohio's 88 counties, making this mode of transportation available to nearly every resident of the state. It became a business that surprisingly lasted into the twentieth century.

There were eventually two major canal systems in Ohio. One, the Ohio and Erie Canal, which started near the mouth of the Cuyahoga River in Cleveland, trekked south through Akron, Coshocton, Newark and Chillicothe, and finally ended at the Ohio River in Portsmouth. The other was the Miami and Erie Canal, which also started at Lake Erie in Toledo and ran down the western side of the Buckeye State through Maumee, Grand Rapids, St. Marys, Piqua, Dayton, and finally, Cincinnati, where it, too, merged into the Ohio River.

But in the late nineteenth century, railroads had begun edging into and across Ohio. This quicker, more accessible means of transportation soon cut into the popularity of the much slower canal system and began choking-off the canal freight business so that by the dawn of the twentieth century, canal operators were making more money selling canal water to businesses and towns that sprang up along their routes than they were making by hauling freight.

The end of the canal era came in 1913 when, after a severe winter with heavy snow, Ohio was hit by a March rainstorm that caused heavy flooding over much of the state. Reservoirs flooded, spilling into canals, smashing out locks, and washing away the banks of the canals. The damage was so devastating that the canals never recovered.

Monticello III Canal Boat Ride. *(Historic Roscoe Village)*

After the floods, much of the damaged canals became weed-choked ditches and were eventually sold off to private individuals or, in some cases, the lands were transferred to other state agencies and used for recreation or made into roads.

Today many communities across the state have restored sections of the old canals as tourist attractions. One of the longest stretches of a water-filled part of the Ohio and Erie Canal runs through the Cuyahoga Valley National Park, which has a visitors center that explains how the canals worked, and you can walk along the actual towpath.

There are four places in Ohio where you can still ride on an authentic canal boat.

In Canal Fulton, south of Akron, from May until late September you can take a replica of a canal boat along a one-mile stretch of the old canal. The *St. Helena III* is a 60-passenger boat based on the freighters that once sailed this canal. The horse-drawn ride takes about an hour for a cruise to Lock IV, where it turns around and comes back to Heritage Park where the ride begins.

One of the best places in Ohio to see what canal life was really like is to visit **Roscoe Village**, a restored canal town on the outskirts of Coshocton, Ohio. Here, businesses that were spawned by the canal or were representative of the canal era still operate with guides in costumes of the time. One of the first re-created canal boats in the state, the *Monticello III*, offers visitors a narrated ride over a mile-and-a-half of the old canal into a turning basin before returning to the park at the edge of town.

In Northwest Ohio, Metroparks Toledo does a good job of demonstrating life on the canals with a ride on their replica canal boat at Providence Park. It's one of the few places in the state where you can go through a working hand-operated lock that raises and lowers the boat. There is also a water-powered grist mill that is part of the park.

In Southwest Ohio, the Ohio Historical Society operates the **Johnston Farm**, a 200-acre park that also includes a portion of the Miami-Erie Canal. Here a 70-foot-long replica of an early canal boat, the *General Harrison*, offers rides to visitors during the summer months.

It's a journey into Ohio's past, and it's just a One Tank Trip.

Johnston Farm and Indian Agency, Piqua Historic District
9845 N Hardin Rd • Piqua, OH   937-773-2522
www.ohiohistory.org

Providence Metropark Canal Experience
13827 U.S. Rte 24 • Grand Rapids, OH   419-407-9741
www.metroparkstoledo.com

Roscoe Village, Roscoe Village Foundation
600 N Whitewoman St • Coshocton, OH   740-622-9310
www.roscoevillage.com

St. Helena Heritage Park
103 Tuscarawas St • Canal Fulton, OH   330-854-6835
www.discovercanalfulton.com

Canal Visitor Center, Cuyahoga Valley National Recreation Area
Canal Rd at Hillside Rd • Valley View, OH   216-524-1497
www.nps.gov

Castles of Ohio

Alliance, Loveland, New Plymouth

We've all heard the famous quotation, "A man's home is his castle." There are some real castles in the Buckeye State, although most are not private homes anymore. Some of these magnificent buildings have turrets, crenellations, and balistraria (slits through the walls and doors so archers defending the castle could fire on invaders). The really fun part is that all of them are open to visitors and tours.

We'll start with perhaps the best-known castle with the most unexpected use: **Glamorgan Castle** in Alliance.

Believe it or not, today the castle is owned by the Alliance city school system.

Despite a legend to the contrary, it was not brought, stone-by-stone, from Wales. The building was the original design of a local architect for the home of Colonel William Morgan, a wealthy Alliance industrialist. The three-story building was constructed of Vermont marble. When it was completed, it contained secret passages, a swimming pool and bowling alley.

Glamorgan Castle has gone through many owners over the years; the next to last being the Alliance Machine Company, which restored the building to its original grandeur, including the installation of a huge crystal chandelier in the main hall that is the duplicate of one presented to the Shah of Iran.

The Alliance School Board purchased the castle in the 1970s with the help of a three-quarters-of-a-million dollar preservation grant. Today it serves as the administrative offices for the schools. The old swimming pool is used for book storage, and a hidden room in the basement, once most likely used for hiding liquor during Prohibition, is now a repository for old school records. You can see this and much of the building by taking a tour on Fridays. Call for a reservation. There is a nominal fee.

When you first approach **Ravenwood Castle**, high on a wooded hill in rural Vinton County near the Hocking Hills of Southeast Ohio, you might start hearing in your mind the strains of the Broadway musical *Camelot*.

Glamogan Castle in Alliance. Once a private home, now the home of the Alliance Schools.

Ravenwood was built in 1994 to replicate a twelfth century European castle. Then- owner Sue Maxwell told me she wanted to create an inn that suggested romantic times, and what could be more romantic than a castle to house knights and their ladies?

This is the only Ohio castle that I have seen that has a faux drawbridge at the entrance. There is a great room with a suit of armor. In addition to the castle with its several regal suites, there is also a "village" outside the castle where there are luxury-filled cottages shaped like medieval homes that offer king-size beds, whirlpool tubs and fireplaces. There are also cabins with modern amenities in a nearby meadow.

Present owners of the castle, Jim and Pam Reed, offer a variety of events at the castle to keep guests coming back, such as murder mystery weekends and a beer tasting. You will want to check out the castle's website to see what they are currently offering.

I've saved the most authentic castle for last. **Chateau La Roche** ("castle of rock") is located in Loveland, Ohio, near Cincinnati. It was the life's-work of a Boy Scout leader and Sunday school teacher named Harry Andrews, who started building it in the 1920s along the banks of the Little Miami River, one river rock at a time, with the help of his scout troop.

He modeled it on medieval castles he had seen when he served in Europe during World War I. It's complete down to the balistraria,

The Loveland Castle, also known as Chateau LaRoche.

narrow winding stairways to turrets, massive oaken doors, stone floors and even a dungeon. It also served as Harry Andrews' home.

The castle today is operated by the Knights of the Golden Trail, an organization formed many years ago by the childless Andrews to honor members of his scout troop who helped build the castle over a 30-year period.

When Andrews died in 1981, a result of burns he received in a grass fire on the castle grounds, his will left the castle to the Knights of the Golden Trail, who still operate the building as a tourist attraction and offer tours year-round.

Chateau La Roche
12025 Shore Rd • Loveland, OH   513-683-4686
www.lovelandcastle.com

Glamorgan Castle
200 Glamorgan St • Alliance, OH   330-821-2100

Ravenwood Castle
65666 Bethel Rd • New Plymouth, OH   800-477-1541
www.ravenwoodcastle.com

Forts of Ohio

Bolivar, Mansfield, Perrysburg, Steubenville

In the early 1800s, Ohio was still considered the western frontier. Much of the land was still wilderness. Forts and blockhouses dotted the state to protect settlers from marauding Native Americans and, at times, from British troops.

As the frontier pushed farther west, and the threat of British invasion eased, people looking for land or a new start poured into Ohio, creating towns and villages. Trails became roads. Railroad tracks and canals brought commerce to and from the state. There was little need for fortifications, and most were allowed to fall into disrepair. Eventually, they were either torn down or plowed under by farmers.

Today, as you travel across the Buckeye State, there are many historical markers that point out where these bastions of safety and protection once stood. And fortunately, in a few cases, re-creations of the original forts have been constructed to remind us of our past.

The most impressive of these fortresses is **Fort Meigs**, on the banks of the Maumee River near Toledo.

Originally built by Gen. William Henry Harrison in 1813 as a supply depot and staging area for a planned invasion of British-controlled Canada, the fort, named for-then-Ohio Gov. Return Jonathan Meigs, Jr., is located on a bluff on the south side of the Maumee River. It was huge, built to house more than 2,000 soldiers. On May 1, 1813, British forces laid siege to the fort for four days before being beaten off by Harrison and his men. In July 1813, the British, accompanied by their Indian allies, again tried to take the fort and once again failed.

After the war, the fort was abandoned and later burned to the ground. Nearly 100 years later in 1904, a memorial marker was erected on the site. In 1967, the Ohio Historical Society began exploring the site and rebuilding the fort, which was opened to the public in 1976. The fort covers 10 acres with blockhouses, barracks, and other buildings inside the stockade. In 2003, a visitors center and museum were added, along with continued reconstruction of the original fort. It is now the largest reconstructed log fort in America.

Fort Steuben. *(Historic Fort Steuben)*

The fort is open from April to October; the visitors center and museum are open year-round.

Fort Laurens, the only fort built by the federal government in Ohio during the Revolutionary War, was also supposed to be rebuilt.

Located in Bolivar, south of Canton, the fort was named for Henry Laurens, president of the Continental Congress.

The one-acre–sized fort was built on the banks of the Tuscarawas River in November 1778. The British and their Native American allies found the fort a threat to their forces in northwestern Ohio, and repeatedly laid siege to the fort throughout the winter. Both sides suffered, many nearly starving to death. The battle ended in March, when the British and Indians withdrew just days before a relief column arrived from Fort Pitt to rescue the beleaguered fort.

Twenty of the defenders killed during the terrible winter battle were buried just outside the fort. In late 1779, President George Washington ordered the fort abandoned.

In 1915, the Ohio legislature passed a bill that allowed the state to purchase the land where Fort Laurens was located, and signified their intent to rebuild the fort as a historical monument. Over 100 years have passed, and the fort still has not been rebuilt.

There is a museum on the spot today with artifacts and maps showing the location of the fort. In 1976, while repaving a road in the park around the museum, workers discovered the body of an unknown defender of the fort. A simple granite tomb now stands in front of what would have been the entrance to the fort. Inscribed on its side are these words:

In this place of honor rests
an unknown soldier who

gave his life in the struggle
for American Independence.

A crypt inside the museum contains the names and remains of the other soldiers who died defending the fort.

The Fort Laurens museum is closed during the winter and is only open from the end of May through Labor Day.

Two blockhouses were built on the square in the city of Mansfield in 1813.

The fear of the British and local Indian forces prompted many frontier communities to build blockhouses, a sort of one-building mini-fort, to give them a place to gather in times of attack. The historic **Mansfield blockhouse** figured in the legend of Johnny Appleseed, the quixotic man who wandered through the Midwest planting apple orchards in the early nineteenth century.

Appleseed, whose real name was John Chapman, was said to have overheard a plan to attack the village of Mansfield by hostile Indians. Chapman allegedly volunteered to run through the nearby woods to alert settlers and urge them to take refuge in the Mansfield blockhouses. It is also said that he ran to a nearby fort and brought back a contingent of soldiers who helped turn away the attack.

One of the two blockhouses has survived the years. It was moved from its location on the square many years ago and taken to a new place, which today is South Park, a city park on the west side of Mansfield. It may well be the only authentic blockhouse still standing in the Midwest.

Fort Steuben, built in the late 1700s to protect surveyors sent to Ohio by the Continental Congress, was rebuilt in 1989 on the original site in downtown Steubenville in southeastern Ohio. Today, the rebuilt fort contains several buildings that depict life in the 1700s, when settlers were pushing into the Ohio River Valley. There are also programs during the summer in which costumed reenactors present living history to visitors.

The visitors center is open year-round; the fort, from May through October.

But a fort that was used in the American Civil War might have the strangest story. Fort Fizzle was a rallying place in bucolic Holmes County where "Copperheads," a group opposed to the draft during the War Between the States, faced off against Union troops sent to take their leaders into custody. Fort Fizzle was actually an old stone house with a tunnel to a nearby orchard. As the federal troops marched toward the fort, someone inside fired at them. The Union soldiers then sounded the charge, and as they approached the walls of the fort, the defenders broke and started running for the woods. The battle was over almost as soon as it started. No one was seriously injured, but the action became the only case of armed rebellion against the Union in Ohio during the war.

And the name, "Fort Fizzle"? Originally, the defenders had called their redoubt Fort Vallandigham in honor of Ohio Congressman Clement Vallandigham, who was known to be a supporter of the Copperheads. But because the battle had ended so quickly, newspapers dubbed the fort "Fort Fizzle," and the name stuck.

Ruins of the old fort are on private property near the intersection of County Road 6 and County Highway 25 near the village of Glenmont. This site is not open to the public.

Fort Meigs
29100 W River Rd • Perrysburg, OH   419-874-4121
www.fortmeigs.org

Fort Laurens
11067 Fort Laurens Rd NW • Bolivar, OH   330-874-2059
fortlaurens.org

Mansfield Blockhouse
South Park, 100 Brinkerhoff Ave • Mansfield, OH   419-755-9819

Fort Steuben
120 S Third St • Steubenville, OH   740-283-1787
www.oldfortsteuben.com

The Lincoln Highway

Bucyrus, Canton, Hanoverton, Van Wert

Did you know that America's first national memorial to Abraham Lincoln is partially located in Ohio?

The Lincoln Highway, America's first coast-to-coast road, ran from New York City to San Francisco, California. It was created in 1913. Nearly 10 years before the Lincoln Memorial in Washington, D.C., was built.

In the early 1900s roads were few and far between. They usually just connected farms to markets and linked some nearby small communities. Outside of cities, roads just seemed to end. There were no state or national highways. Some small rural communities were completely isolated in the early twentieth century.

That all changed in 1913. Three men—Henry Joy of the Packard Automobile Company, Frank Seiberling of Goodyear Tire and Rubber Company, and Carl Fisher, a maker of headlights for cars—were instrumental in forming the Lincoln Highway Association.

Their idea was to create a highway across America as a memorial to the slain Civil War president and to form one route that would take travelers from the Atlantic to the Pacific coast.

Obviously, they also hoped that the road would encourage more people to buy automobiles. What they succeeded in doing was to establish a continuous ribbon of road across the United States.

Some parts of the new road were brick, other areas were made from cement, gravel and, in some cases, graded dirt. But it was the first time a single road had spanned our country.

The Ohio part of the Lincoln Highway begins where it leaves Pennsylvania and enters the state in East Liverpool and snakes its way across the north central portion of the Buckeye State, closely following what is today U.S. Route 30.

It passes through Lisbon, Minerva, Canton, Massillon, Wooster, Ashland and Mansfield. From there it jogs through Crestline, Bucyrus, Upper Sandusky, Delphos and leaves Ohio on the western side of Van Wert and enters the state of Indiana.

A great One Tank Trip any time of year is to explore portions of this

A modern-day Lincoln driving on the Lincoln Highway. This is one of the few remaining original stretches of the Lincoln Highway near Canton.

historic roadway. One stretch that truly captures the essence of the original Lincoln Highway is the area from Hanoverton to Minerva, east of Canton.

Near Robertsville you will find Bayard Road. This brick two-lane roadway is unchanged from the early twentieth century when it was built and is just wide enough to accommodate two passing Model "T" automobiles. An occasional farm dots the rural landscape, and as the road rolls up and down hills, there are incredible views of the surrounding countryside, some of it the same as it has been for more than a century. On a nearby utility pole, the red, white and blue logo with a large blue "L" identifies this as part of the original Lincoln Highway.

As you enter the town of Minerva, there is another artifact of the original highway, seemingly frozen in time: an old gasoline station at the corner of Market Street and Lincoln Way. While it now serves as a gift shop, you can still see the old glass-topped gasoline pumps and the unmistakable architecture of an early twentieth century service station.

The building also served as a control station on the Lincoln Highway. In those early days, there were no electronic road navigation systems in the automobiles. Road maps were almost non-existent. Printed directions from the Lincoln Highway Association gave exact mileage, directions and landmarks from one town to another. When you reached a control station, you reset your odometer to zero for the next lap.

One of the markers for the Lincoln
Highway placed by Boy Scouts in 1928.

The Lincoln Highway was not the only means of major transportation in this area at that time The Sandy and Beaver Canal, a spur off
the larger Ohio-Erie Canal, passed through the town of Hanoverton.

The historic town of Hanoverton has seen it all. Homes on Plymouth Street date back to the early 1800s, when the canal was built.
Here you 'l still find the **Spread Eagle Tavern and Inn**, one of the most
popular fine dining restaurants in Columbiana County and a luxurious place to spend the night while touring the Lincoln Highway.

The Spread Eagle was built in 1837. It has three floors, 11 rooms and
12 fireplaces. There are seven dining rooms ranging from the formal
William McKinley Room, named for the former U.S. president who
once stayed here, to a more informal "barn room" which appears to
be the inside of a log cabin.

Head east on the Lincoln Highway and you'll reach Canton, where
you can see more of the history of the famous road at the **Canton
Classic Car Museum**, which also is linked to the Lincoln Highway.

Brothers George and Joseph Sacher opened a bicycle shop in the
building in 1913. But when they discovered the nation's first coast-
to-coast highway was going through their city, they quickly changed
their business to automobile repair and became a necessary stop on
the Lincoln Highway. Today, the Canton Classic Car Museum has a
small exhibit dedicated to the early days of the Lincoln Highway, with
signs, pictures, maps and brochures.

The Lincoln Highway passes through downtown Bucyrus in Crawford County. Be sure to stop and see one of Ohio's most unusual war memorials: **"Liberty Remembers,"** a mural painted by famed painter Eric Grohe. It is 36 feet wide and 44 feet high, painted on the side of a building, and depicts the figure of Liberty holding a dying soldier wrapped in an American flag. But when you look closer, you'll see the faces of 284 Crawford County veterans, ranging from the Revolutionary War to the Gulf War, blended into the mural. And if you look very closely, you will even see a four-legged veteran of the Vietnam War, Nemo, a member of the canine corps.

When you reach Van Wert on the western edge of Ohio, the Lincoln Highway takes you past another building that was a significant "first" in Ohio: the **Brumback Library**. It is historically important because back in 1901, when it was completed, it became the very first county-supported library in the U.S.

But there is another reason you might want to make a stop and explore. The library building looks like a castle. The unusual architecture is a combination of Romanesque and Gothic styles, with tile roofs and turreted towers.

If you stick to the old original roads that made up America's first transcontinental road, the Lincoln Highway, it is more than 240 miles from East Liverpool on the Pennsylvania state line to Van Wert on the Indiana border.

Spread Eagle Tavern and Inn
10150 Plymouth St • Hanoverton, OH   330-223-1583
www.spreadeagletavern.com

Canton Classic Car Museum
123 Sixth St SW • Canton, OH   330-456-3603
www.cantonclassiccar.org

"Liberty Remembers" Memorial Mural
203 N Sandusky Ave • Bucyrus, OH   419-562-4811
www.bucyrusohio.com

Brumback Library
215 W Main St • Van Wert, OH   419-238-2168
www.brumbacklib.com

Ohio Lincoln Highway Historic Byway
PO Box 20509 • Canton, OH   419-468-6773
www.dot.state.oh.us/OhioByways/Pages/LincolnHighway.aspx

Holiday Lights in Ohio

Cambridge, Coshocton, East Cleveland, Wooster

Free is good. I like anything free. Sadly, you can't always do things that are free. Even really good "free" attractions will cost something. It might be the gasoline to get there, food along the way for you and the family, or the cost of a souvenir. With that in mind, here are some recommendations for the holiday seasons.

Down through the years, my family has usually gone to see the lights of the holidays in downtown Cleveland.

When I was a youngster, there were always the windows in the Higbee Department Store on Public Square, as shown in the movie, *A Christmas Story*. Even now, a drive through downtown is usually a great way to get the season off to a start. From the lights on the Terminal Tower to the blaze of colored lights and the activities on Public Square, a drive down Euclid Avenue through the Playhouse Square District, with its magnificent chandelier, has become a new tradition for many families.

You can extend this drive out to **Nela Park** in East Cleveland. The Noble Road site is the world headquarters of GE's Lighting Division, and each year for more than 90 years, they have illuminated the park-like setting of this industrial site. Among the thousands of lights and displays, Nela Park usually has a replica of the tree they decorate each year for the White House in Washington, D.C.

If you are not up to fighting big city traffic, remember that even small towns usually have their own holiday traditions.

The city of Wooster in Wayne County, for example, encourages local stores to create animated displays celebrating the holiday season. Wooster also claims to have a historical connection to the erection of the first Christmas tree in Ohio. Legend has it that in 1847 August Imgard, a local tailor, was homesick for the Christmas trees that his family had had in his native Bavaria. He cut down a tree and erected it in his brother's home. It was a sensation with local folks, and the next year, many people in Wooster and other communities copied Imgard's tree.

The house where Imgard put up the first Christmas tree still stands.

Holiday candle-lighting ceremony at Roscoe Village. *(Roscoe Village Foundation)*

Today, it is the rectory of St. Mary's Church. A huge, lighted Christmas tree also is set up in the Wooster Cemetery in front of August Imgard's tomb.

To get into the spirit of a Victorian Christmas, then drive to Cambridge, Ohio, during the holidays. The whole town pays homage to Charles Dickens, the man who wrote *A Christmas Carol*. In the **Dickens Victorian Village**, more than 90 mannequins dressed in authentic Victorian costumes are displayed throughout the downtown. There are carriage rides, and each evening during the festival, the Guernsey County Courthouse in the heart of the city comes alive with the lights and sounds of the season.

Roscoe Village, the restored canal town in Coshocton, Ohio, is a great One Tank Trip during the holiday season.

Walking down the main street of the village is like traveling back in time. Women in hoop skirts and bonnets smile as they pass by. Men in top hats join together under streetlights to sing Christmas carols. Candles glow from the windows of restored homes, stores, and warehouses along what was once a port on the Ohio and Erie Canal.

The area known as Roscoe Village was rescued from oblivion back in the early 1960s by businessman Edward Montgomery and his wife, Frances. They became interested in the history of the defunct canal and started a personal project of restoring old homes and businesses, one at a time.

Their work grew into the Roscoe Village Foundation that today includes not only the town, but a working one-mile section of the Ohio Erie Canal with an authentic horse-drawn canal boat, the *Monticello III*, that offers rides during the summer season. The village is open year-round with a full schedule of special events.

Every Saturday night during the month of December, the village holds a candle-lighting ceremony in the center of town. Some years ago, I was privileged to be the official "candle-lighter," and it became a special holiday memory for me and my family.

The program begins on a stage in the center of the village.

On a hillside beyond the stage stands a darkened 35-foot-tall Christmas tree. The street and the hillside are filled with hundreds of visitors.

A choir from the community softly sings holiday music, and the crowd joins in. A special Christmas story is read, then the candle-lighter lights his or her candle and walks to the edges of the stage where dozens of hands proffer unlit candles and touches his flame to each of the outstretched hands. They, in turn, light the candles of those around them. The candle glow sweeps steadily across the crowd and up the hillside, and at the same instant, the huge Christmas tree suddenly blazes in light. It is truly a magical moment.

If you come to spend the day, most of the stores are open, offering crafts, foods, and more, and a look at the world as it was a century ago. There are carriage rides, cider warmed over an open fire, and the smell of chestnuts roasting and freshly-made hot ginger cookies. Roscoe Village is a place where you can do some holiday shopping and take home a bagful of memories.

Dickens Victorian Village
Wheeling Ave • Cambridge, OH   800-933-5480
www.dickensvictorianvillage.com

Nela Park
GE Lighting, 1975 Noble Rd, East Cleveland, OH

Roscoe Village Foundation
600 N Whitewoman St • Coshocton, OH   800-877-1830
www.roscoevillage.com

Wayne County Convention & Visitors Bureau
428 W Liberty St • Wooster, OH   330-264-6474
www.wccvb.com

Holiday Train Rides

If you have children or grandchildren, the **Cuyahoga Valley Scenic Railroad** is a place to make some new family holiday memories.

For openers, the kids can take a ride with Santa Claus and Mr. Jingeling, (Santa's number-one elf and keeper of the keys) through the historic Cuyahoga Valley National Recreational Area.

The Santa Claus and Mr. Jingeling Express runs on just one weekend in late November.

You also can take the train to pick out your Christmas tree. In fact, you get both a train and a trolley ride to Heritage Farms in Peninsula, where you can cut your own tree, or select a pre-cut tree. While you have lunch at one of the local restaurants, the farm staff tags, bags, and places your tree on the train for the return trip to Independence. These trips are popular and fill up fast, so reservations are important. The Christmas Tree Adventure rides are also held on the last weekend in November.

But the really big event each holiday season is the Polar Express run.

It has become so popular that it sells out almost as soon as it is announced each year.

The ride brings to life the Chris Van Allsburg book that tells the story of the little boy who dreams of taking a train trip to the North Pole to see Santa Claus.

Kids and adults are invited to wear their pajamas as they board the heated train along with elves and other holiday characters for an evening adventure to the "North Pole." This event might also sell out before December, so make your reservations as soon as possible.

Another popular Polar Express train ride is in Dennison, Ohio, at the historic **Dennison Depot**.

The adventure starts here as you board the train. Elves greet, read stories to the kids, and offer them fresh-baked cookies from Mrs. Claus along with some special elfin hot-chocolate.

When the train arrives at the North Pole, you watch as more elves gather trackside to meet you. You can see into Santa's workshop, and Santa comes aboard for the ride back to Dennison.

One advantage of the Dennison Polar Express, is that, for an extra fee, you can buy "first class" seating. That means if it is a cold blustery night, you don't have to wait outside for the train. You go to the "first class" waiting room inside the depot, where the conductor will seat you first when the train arrives.

Both rides are extremely popular and sell out quickly, so make your reservations early.

Cuyahoga Valley Scenic Railroad
PO Box 158 • Peninsula, OH   800-468-4070
www.cvsr.com

Dennison Railroad Depot and Baggage Room
400 Center St • Dennison, OH   740-922-6776
www.dennisondepot.org

CENTRAL OHIO

The Whistleblower of Columbus

Columbus

Ray Giesse is quite literally Ohio's number-one whistleblower.

You see, Ray owns the **American Whistle Corporation**, the last manufacturer of metal whistles in the entire country.

His little one-story factory on the north side of Columbus turns out thousands of the whistles every day.

On one of our visits Giesse told me that just about everyone can use one of his whistles, from senior citizens, who carry them to call for help, to amateur coaches and referees. Many police officers throughout Ohio carry whistles from American Whistle as part of their uniform.

I have always been curious: How do they get that little ball in the whistle to make the shrill, distinctive sound when it's blown?

According to Ray, the ball is actually made from cork, compressed by a special machine, and inserted into the body of the whistle. When it is released, it returns to its spherical shape.

When I was a youngster one of the rites of passage in junior high school was the field trips we took to local factories to see how things were made.

Sadly, more and more factories have discontinued the practice because of safety requirements and other legal reasons.

I am happy to report that American Whistle still welcomes visitors

A presentation whistle made for the Super Bowl by American Whistle Corporation.

to their plant. Tours are by appointment and only during hours of production. They like to have groups of 15 or more, but even if you don't have a group you can be added to a tour. There is no age limit, and every visitor leaves with a shiny, classic American Whistle.

One of the neat things you will learn, besides how they get the ball into the whistle, is that each year, American Whistle makes presentation whistles for the officials of the Super Bowl. The whistles are gold-plated and packed in a wooden presentation box.

If you have a coach or referee in your family, you can buy a copy of the gold presentation whistle at the company store after your visit.

If you will excuse the pun, this is a story where you whistle while you work.

American Whistle Corporation
6540 Huntley Rd #B • Columbus, OH   614-846-2918
www.americanwhistle.com

For more things to see and do in the Columbus area, see other chapters in this book or:

Experience Columbus
www.experiencecolumbus.com   614-221-6623

Politicians and Peanut Butter

Columbus

If you have followed my adventures for very long, you know that I like to do things that are free. Free is good.

In Columbus you can get a free guided tour of the historic **Ohio Statehouse**. You might even bump into the governor or one of our legislators. You never know.

Seriously, the capitol building has been beautifully renovated and the tours can be very interesting for both children and adults.

In the rotunda you will learn that the statehouse was originally built by convicts from the state penitentiary.

Also, the famed painting Commodore Perry and the Battle of Lake Erie that hangs in the rotunda was used by the artist to force the state to pay him more than they had initially agreed to pay. You see, after he completed the painting, he took it on tour, including a trip to Washington, D.C. When members of Congress saw it, they wanted it for the U.S. Capitol. A bidding war ensued, and the artist won. Ohio finally got the painting at a much higher price—then the artist painted a nearly identical version and sold it to Congress for the U.S. Capitol.

The governor's Ceremonial Office in the Statehouse is usually available for tours, if the governor isn't using it for meetings.

There is also a gift shop where you can buy Ohio-themed souvenirs. It's located near the map room in the basement. The map room is so-named because every county in Ohio is carved into the stone floor.

A newly opened Statehouse Museum includes state-of-the-art technology that allows visitors to experience through virtual reality the roles that the governor and legislators play in our lives.

Guided tours of the building are available on the hour from 10:00 a.m. until 3:00 p.m., Monday through Friday, and from noon until 3:00 p.m. on Saturdays and Sundays.

Unless you suffer from arachibutyrophobia (that's the scientific term for people who fear peanut butter sticking to the roof of their mouth), this trip may be the perfect family One Tank Trip.

While in Columbus you can get a really good peanut butter and jelly sandwich at **Krema Nut Company**.

The Ohio statehouse.

Incidentally, it's claimed that G.I.s in World War II developed the PB&J when they started mixing the almost inedible C-ration peanut butter with the packaged jelly to make it more palatable. The quality of peanut butter has come a long way since then.

Krema happens to be the oldest peanut butter company in the country.

It was over 100 years ago that Benton Black ground his first batch of peanuts to make Krema Peanut Butter.

The company still makes pure peanut butter: no oils, no salt, no additives, just peanuts ground into a buttery consistency.

It's probably the healthiest brand you can eat, and it tastes good, too. And get this: You can buy it right at the factory, along with various kinds of nuts and candy and they have also installed a sandwich bar where you can purchase a custom-made PB&J sandwich.

The menu features 13 varieties including the "Classic Old Timer," which contains chunky peanut butter, strawberry preserves, and sliced strawberries; "Grandma's Apple Pie," which combines creamy peanut butter and an apple fruit spread; and my favorite, "PB Apple Cheesecake," which spreads creamy peanut butter, honey, nuts, and cream cheese on one slice of bread and lots of chunky apple preserves on the other slice.

There are large windows from the store into the factory where you

A really good PB&J from the sandwich bar at Krema Nut Company. *(Krema Nut Company)*

can watch peanut butter being made. They do not run the production line on weekends, and the factory store is closed on Sunday.

Krema Nut Company
1000 Goodale Blvd • Columbus, OH   614-299-4131
www.krema.com

Statehouse Tours
The Ohio Statehouse • 1 Capitol Square • Columbus, OH   614-752-9777
www.ohiostatehouse.org

For more suggestions in the Columbus and central Ohio area, see other chapters in this book or contact the local tourism bureau:

Experience Columbus
www.experiencecolumbus.com   614-221-6623

The Charm of Charm

Charm, Millersburg

Believe it or not, I have been to Charm School.

I didn't attend the school; I was just visiting. And, no, it was not that kind of charm school. It was Charm School, an elementary school in Charm, Ohio.

I can hear the moans. But just about everybody who drives through Charm, in Holmes County, stops to take a picture outside of the Charm School.

Charm and the Doughty Valley in the surrounding townships have always been one of my favorite places in Ohio's Amish Country.

I count Eric and Julia Guggisberg among my friends. While they are not Amish, their heritage, like mine, is Swiss. Eric's father, the late Albert Guggisberg, created "Baby Swiss Cheese," which the family still sells at their factory, The Guggisberg Cheese Company, just down the road.

Across the highway is the family-operated Chalet-in-the-Valley Restaurant that specializes in Swiss, Bavarian and Austrian foods.

Eric and Julia own the Guggisberg Swiss Inn, a charming place that reminds you of a chalet tucked away in the Alps, except for all the horses, which you'll find grazing in pastures stretching over the rolling countryside.

Eric has had a lifelong interest in horses and operates one of the few stables in the area that offers horseback riding to the public.

His **Amish Country Riding Stables** specialize in trail-rides for groups of two to five that give riders a unique look at the Amish countryside.

The stables also offer buggy rides and, when the weather permits, horse-drawn sleigh rides. Eric doesn't allow wheels on his sleighs, so conditions have to be just right, with a snow depth of at least four inches to enable the horse and sleigh to move at a gallop over the snow.

Wrapped in a warm robe, sitting on a velvet seat in the sleigh, you feel like a living Currier and Ives lithograph. Eric sits in front and gives the horse the command to go. Suddenly you are flying over the snow, flakes sticking to your eyelashes and hair. The snow-covered beauty

Horses waiting for riders at Amish Country Riding Stables. *(Eric Guggisberg)*

of the hillside near the inn flashes by, and all you hear are the sleigh bells and the rhythmic thud of the horses' hooves.

It is one of those experiences that creates a memory that lasts a lifetime.

Amish Country Riding Stables
5025 State Rte 557 • Millersburg, OH   330-893-3600
www.guggisbergswissinn.com

There are a lot more Swiss- and Amish-influenced sites in this area. For similar attractions, see other chapters in this book or:

Holmes County Chamber of Commerce and Tourism Bureau
www.visitamishcountry.com • 330-674-3975

Bats in Ohio

Plain City

Okay, sports fans, you all know what a Louisville Slugger is, but did you know that there is an Ohio company that also makes baseball bats so good that they are used by major league baseball players?

If you thought that all professional baseball bats were made in Louisville, Kentucky, you might be surprised to learn that there are over 30 baseball bat–making companies nationwide approved to make bats for the major leagues. Phoenix Bats in Plain City is the only one in Ohio.

Phoenix Bats began because company founder Charles Trudeau liked to play baseball as they did in the 1860s. He is a member of the Columbus, Ohio, Village Muffins, a team sponsored by the Ohio Historical Society, who play against other, similar teams using replica equipment and the rules of baseball as the game originally was played shortly after the American Civil War.

Trudeau, whose livelihood was restoring old homes, loved working with wood and wanted an historically-correct bat from the 1860s. The rules of the time stated the barrel of the bat could be no bigger around than 2.5 inches, but could be as long as the bat creator wanted to make it. So he went to the wood lathe in his garage and, using pictures and drawings from the period, created his own bat.

His fellow players admired the finished product, and soon he was getting requests to make bats for other teams across the state. Eventually, the demand led to a bat-making business. As his business grew, Trudeau had to decide whether to go full-time into bat-making. "Twenty years from now," he said, "I didn't want to look back and wonder, was I good enough to have my bats in the top level of baseball, the major leagues," he recalls.

So in the spring of 2000, Trudeau went to the Cleveland Indians spring training camp with an armload of bats that he asked Indian players to try. Infielder John McDonald tried one and soon ordered some bats from Phoenix, becoming the first major league player to use an Ohio-made bat.

Trudeau says proudly, "Today we have our bats being used by

The only bat maker in Ohio approved to make bats for the major leagues. *(Phoenix Bats)*

players in almost every major league team in the country, but I will always remember John McDonald for being the first."

Today the company makes both youth and adult bats.

They have a store at the front of their plant where examples of their bats and related products are on display.

It was this store and the number of baseball fans coming into the plant that made Phoenix a Plain City tourist attraction.

Trudeau says, "We have a window in the store that looks into the production area, and people kept asking to go back to watch the bats being made." So the company started offering a plant tour for a modest fee that includes a small souvenir bat at the end of the 45-minute tour. "Now we get busloads of tourists stopping," Trudeau adds.

The plant isn't that large, and it is mostly automated, but for a true baseball fan, it is a place to see a block of wood turned, step-by-step, into a polished, engraved baseball bat ready to take to the field.

Phoenix Bats
7801 Corporate Blvd • Plain City, OH   614-873-7776
www.phoenixbats.com

For more nearby attractions, see other chapters in this book or:

TourismOhio
www.ohio.org   1-800-BUCKEYE

Hot Mustard and Wedding Gowns

West Lafayette

There's this unique store in central Ohio. It is a little place that grew and grew and is still growing. It is the kind of a spot where you can buy a really good sandwich and your wedding gown.

You can also get a great hamburger, have your photo taken on the original set of the TV show, "The Price is Right," and take home some 50 different kinds of mustard or dozens and dozens of different kinds of cheese.

It is a most unusual shopping complex that even has a tiny wedding chapel where you can get married.

It's called **Unusual Junction**, and it's located in West Lafayette in Coshocton County.

The family-owned business was started by patriarch Jerry McKenna more than 35 years ago.

Formerly of North Olmsted, Jerry bought the West Lafayette property on which to build a small roadside stand where he could sell antiques on weekends.

McKenna, whose background was in construction, later bought the abandoned railroad station in Fredericktown, 70 miles away, moved it to his property along U.S. Route 36 and reassembled it, adding two cabooses, one on each end of the station, because, as he puts it, "We didn't know which way we were going."

The roadside stand morphed into a restaurant/delicatessen/antique store because Jerry says when people were shopping and asked where they could get something to eat, the nearest restaurant was miles away. He says, "I didn't want them leaving. I was afraid they might not come back."

The addition to the site of some old railroad passenger cars 25 years ago prompted Jerry and his family to turn one of the cars into a small store selling bridal gowns and offering tuxedo rentals because there was no similar store for miles around.

The idea really caught on, and today The Universe Bridal and Prom fills an entire new wing next to the old depot.

Inside, you will find a selection of more than 1,500 bridal gowns.

This prop from the famous TV game show is one of the attractions inside Unusual Junction. *(Junction Enterprises)*

They also offer a staggering selection of more than 5,000 prom and bridesmaid dresses in a rainbow of styles and colors.

They have become one of the largest bridal gown stores in the entire state. But it is the other things you find at Unusual Junction that bring in not only brides, but tour buses loaded with customers.

In the adjoining Lava Rock Grille, decorated with 1950s memorabilia, you can get an oversized ham sandwich or a hamburger made with fresh Black Angus beef. The soups, many made from family recipes, are delicious.

You will also find the huge sign that was used as a backdrop on the TV show, "The Price is Right," along with an autograph of the former host, Bob Barker. Jerry's son Bob bought it online as part of a benefit for a Hollywood charity. "He paid about $3,500 for it," Jerry says, "and it cost us almost that much to have it shipped here."

Also in the dining room is the famous giant three-dimensional mural by artist Tom Miller that once was a fixture in the Alpine-Alpa Restaurant in Wilmot, Ohio. Jerry bought the mural at an auction when that restaurant closed, moved it to his grille, and restored it so that tiny cattle still appear to be marching down from the mountains across a stone bridge under which real water cascades to another level.

"The brides and our customers love to pose for pictures in front of the 'Price is Right' sign and the Amish mural," Jerry says.

Unusual Junction's relocated and repurposed railroad station. *(Junction Enterprises)*

The attached delicatessen, located in the old railroad depot, is also an attraction. Along with locally produced Amish cheeses and meats, the deli sells more than 500 brands of fiery hot sauces and more than 50 flavors of mustard. In fact, in the grille they offer customers a choice of 15 different mustards for their sandwiches.

Jerry has added yet another attraction, a small chapel with only one pew. "That's so every wedding is standing room only," Jerry explains. The tiny chapel holds about a dozen people, most of them standing, and has been the site of numerous weddings.

Jerry and his family have also expanded to nearby Roscoe Village, where they own several businesses.

With a nearby winery as well as a riverside bed and breakfast, Unusual Junction has become one of my favorite One Tank Trips.

Unusual Junction
56310 US Rte 36 • West Lafayette, OH   740-545-9772
www.theunusualjunction.com

For more ideas of places to stay and things to do, check out:

Coshocton Visitors Bureau
www.visitcoshocton.com   740-622-4877

The Bicycles of New Bremen

If, when you were growing up you owned a favorite bicycle, odds are you can find it in New Bremen, Ohio.

New Bremen is not exactly a major crossroads. Tucked away near the Indiana-Ohio border, it's just a dot on the map, 12 miles across flat farmland from the nearest major highway. Until a dozen or so years ago, it was one of those forgotten towns that grew up along the old Miami and Erie Canal. These towns, situated off the beaten path, pretty much dried up after the canals were replaced by railroads and highways as the major means of transportation in Ohio.

But New Bremen, settled mostly by German immigrant-farmers, hung on. Today it looks like a Disney-created village, but it is real.

The town's transformation happened some years ago when Crown Equipment Corporation came to town. Crown's owner, Jim Dicke, had already saved much of the historic downtown by restoring and converting empty circa-1890 store buildings into offices for his sprawling corporation, the town's biggest employer. In 1997, he decided that New Bremen needed a world-class tourist attraction.

So he went to Chicago, where the famous Schwinn Bicycle Company was selling off its huge collection of antique bikes.

Dicke started bidding, and by the end of the day, he was the owner of most of the collection. He hauled it back to New Bremen and set up the **Bicycle Museum of America** in an old furniture store, filling more than 14,000 square feet with 350 historic bicycles. It's now the world's largest bicycle museum. Stored in Crown's warehouse are another 1,000 bicycles that are rotated into the museum's displays, with more arriving all the time.

A spokesman told me that most visitors want to see the bicycle they had when they were growing up. Chances are, there's one just like it in the collection.

"There has been little change in the basic design of the bicycle over the past one hundred years," said a tour guide, "But people are constantly coming up with innovations, and we have some of the most unusual examples."

The first thing you see when you enter is a veritable wall of classic bicycles.

For instance, the lightest bike in the collection is a Lynskey that weighs only seven pounds. It can be picked up with just two fingers.

One of the most expensive bicycles in the collection is a tandem specially made for the personal use of the Schwinn family. It cost about $130 to make in the 1890s; Dicke paid $108,000 for it in 1997.

A strange looking bicycle with a huge chain sprocket holds the title of the fastest bicycle ever made. Specially constructed for the Schwinn Company in 1941, it was ridden by Alfred Le Tourner on the Salt Flats of Utah behind a midget automobile racing car to cut down wind resistance. Le Tourner pedaled the bicycle to an incredible 108 miles per hour.

In addition, there are bicycles that were dropped by parachute in World War II and used by airborne troopers. Another bicycle used by the army was in 1891 when a troop of African-American soldiers were equipped with specially built Columbia bicycles and sent on a mission to see whether bikes could replace horses in the U.S. Cavalry. The experiment was to ride across much of the American West, nearly 2,000 miles. The soldiers did it, but despite impressive speeds, the horse was not replaced until the advent of armored tanks.

There are many unusual bicycles in the collection, such as a Harley Davidson model from 1917 that resembles a motorcycle with a side-car.

Probably the biggest modern production bicycle on display is the "Monster Bike," made by Coker Tire in Tennessee. Its tires are 36 inches in diameter, and the whole bike weighs 60 pounds. It dwarfs most adults.

There are other things to do while visiting the bicycle museum. For example, guests are allowed to climb on a six-foot-tall "big wheel" antique bicycle to have their picture taken. In addition, there are hands-on exhibits that demonstrate the difference in performance between the parts used in early bicycles and the space-age materials some bikes are made from today. There's even an adult-size pedal car that you can climb into and tool around the floor.

But it is the everyday bicycle collection that is the star, says a guide. "I've had grown men come in here and see the bicycle they owned as a child and break into tears," he adds.

Visit the Bicycle Museum of America. It's well worth the time.

The Bicycle Museum of America
7 W Monroe St • New Bremen, OH   419-629-9249
www.bicyclemuseum.com

If you want to spend more time in the area, check out the local tourism and visitors bureau for ideas:

Greater Grand Lake Visitors Region
www.seemore.org   419-394-1294

John Glenn's Home Town

New Concord, Norwich

We all have personal heroes. One of mine is John Glenn.

Small towns in Ohio seem to have a history of producing great men and women, and New Concord, Ohio, is such a place.

John Glenn has burned his name into the history books: U.S. Marine, test pilot, astronaut, first American to orbit the earth, U.S. Senator, and an unsuccessful presidential candidate. He capped his amazing career at age 77 by becoming the oldest human to venture into space, this time, as a member of the space shuttle *Discovery* Crew.

His early boyhood home in New Concord, Ohio, is now the **John and Annie Glenn Historic Site and Exploration Center**. The house, built by Glenn's father in 1923, has been restored to its appearance from the late 1930s and 1940s, when John and Annie Glenn were growing up in this small college town.

Instead of a musty, small-town museum, the community here has created a living-history lesson for visitors. Reenactors populate the first floor and take you back to the days of World War II, when nearly every family had someone in the service, represented by a blue star hanging in the window.

The day I visited the home, a reenactor was portraying Clara Glenn, John's mother, in 1943. Wearing an apron and a house dress from the 1940s, she invited us into the kitchen, pointing to rationing books the family used to buy meat, sugar, shoes, and gasoline. She told how she used to babysit both John and a neighbor's daughter, Annie Castor, by keeping them in the same playpen in the kitchen as she worked.

The actor noted they had grown and married each other, and that John was a Marine Corps pilot fighting in the South Pacific.

In the living room, she pointed to the radio that broadcast the news of the day and lovingly showed us pictures of the-then-newlyweds, John and Annie Glenn.

Along with the story of the Glenns, the reenactor wove into the story how a town and nation sacrificed and pulled together to get through the war. It is also a tale of how small-town Ohio values affected the lives of the people who grew up in it.

John Glenn's boyhood home is now a living history museum where you can experience the small town values Glenn was raised on.

On the third floor of the home are four bedrooms, two of which were used by the senior Glenns to add to their income by renting to students at nearby Muskingum College. The other two housed young John Glenn and his adopted sister Jean. John's room is filled with model airplanes, just like the ones he built and collected while growing up.

In a newer section built onto the rear of the home, used for an elevator and gathering room for visitors, there is a small museum that focuses on Glenn's participation in the Space Age.

On the first floor, which is really the basement level, there is the visitors center and entrance. Here you can see a short film about the Glenns narrated by legendary TV journalist Hugh Downs.

The John and Annie Glenn Historic Site is a tasteful tribute not only to the Glenns, but to small-town Ohio.

In fact the road that runs by the Glenn home also was important to the founding of Ohio and the Midwest. It's the subject of another museum in the next community to the west, which is also now operated by the John and Annie Glenn Historic Site.

The **National Road–Zane Grey Museum** in Norwich, Ohio, follows the development of the nation's first "highway" that ran from Cumberland, Maryland, west through Ohio to Vandalia, Illinois.

Through the use of dioramas, models, and old pictures, the museum demonstrates how a simple Indian trail grew from a path into a modern four-lane highway. The museum also honors author Zane Grey, from nearby Zanesville, who was famous for his many western novels.

John and Annie Glenn Historic Site
7268 W Main St • New Concord, OH   740-826-0220
www.johnglennhome.org

National Road–Zane Grey Museum
8850 E Pike • Norwich, OH   740-872-3143
www.ohionationalroad.org

For more ideas in this area, contact:

Cambridge/Guernsey County Visitors & Convention Bureau
www.visitguernseycounty.com   740-432-2022

Zanesville-Muskingum County Convention & Visitors Bureau
www.visitzanesville.com   800-743-2303

Ohio's Floating Island

Hebron

There is an amazing piece of property in Ohio that floats. **Cranberry Bog State Nature Preserve** on Buckeye Lake, near Newark, Ohio, is a one-of-a-kind island that, sadly, some environmentalists say is fast disappearing.

First, a bit of history on how this island came to be.

Almost 200 years ago Ohio decided to build a canal across the state from Lake Erie to the Ohio River. They dammed up streams feeding a large swamp near Newark and created a feeder lake to supply water to the canal.

When the water covered the swamp, creating Buckeye Lake, a large section of mossy bog, about 50 acres, broke loose and floated to the surface. Over the years, the wind and birds have brought other vegetation and even trees to the island. However, erosion continuously attacks the fragile island, and it is now down to about eight acres. Some say it might disappear entirely before the end of this century.

Currently, the island is a treasure chest for environmentalists. Not only does it hold fields of cranberries for which it is named, there are also rare orchids that bloom each summer and two kinds of carnivorous plants. Visitors are warned not to touch any of the plants because the island is also home to poison sumac, which can cause burning and blistering.

The day we visited the island, a guide demonstrated just how unusual the sponge-like earth is to walk on by jumping up and down, causing the earth to shake. Guests on the island are restricted to a boardwalk that winds through the trees and meadows. The island has been a state nature preserve since 1973.

In fact, until a few years ago, visits to the island were very restricted. The Ohio Department of Natural Resources used to hold an annual lottery to allow only 400 visitors per year on the fragile island. In recent years, management of the island has been taken over by the Greater Buckeye Lake Historical Society (GBLHS). One of the first things they did was to take down many trees on the edge of the island that were in danger of shearing off parts of the island if they were blown down in a

Cranberry Bog, the floating island. *(Buckeye Lake Historical Society, courtesy Explore Licking County)*

storm or died of old age and fell into the lake. In addition they lobbied for a "no wake" zone around the island to reduce erosion from waves caused by passing motor boats.

The GBLHS also bought a large pontoon boat that gave guided tours of the island, using guides trained by environmentalists.

However, in 2014 government agencies found a weakness in the dam forming Buckeye Lake and ordered water levels lowered to winter levels year-round, effectively cutting off most boating activity on the already shallow lake until a solution can be found, which may take several years. That order, unfortunately, also stopped boat tours to Cranberry Island.

You can still see the island from the shore, and the **Greater Buckeye Lake Historical Society** museum in nearby Buckeye Lake has many photos and exhibits telling the island's story.

Greater Buckeye Lake Historical Society
4729 Walnut Rd • Hebron, OH   740-929-1998
www.buckeyelakehistory.org

For other attractions or places to stay, contact:

Licking County Convention & Visitors Bureau
www.explorelc.org • 740-345-8224

Fried Bologna and Sky High Pie

Waldo

Just about anywhere I make a public appearance I can count on a question: "Where's that place with the fried bologna sandwich?"

While I didn't set out to do a book on road food, there are certain places that have become so popular that they have indeed become One Tank Trip destinations.

Such a place is Waldo, Ohio.

Actually it is the **G & R Tavern** (named for founders George Yake and Roy Klingel) in Waldo, home to what they claim is the "famous bologna sandwich."

The little working man's bar has been attracting people from all over Ohio for more than a half-century because of their fried bologna made from a secret recipe just for the tavern. It is sliced into thick, half-inch slabs that go on a hot grill until both sides are browned. It is then topped with a slice of Monterey jack cheese that is allowed to melt just enough. The bologna is placed on a kaiser roll and topped with a slice of sweet onion and some crispy dill pickle chips.

Trust me. This is not your mother's fried bologna. People have driven from as far away as Las Vegas to have one of the G & R fried bologna sandwiches.

The current owners, Joy and Bernie Lewis and their friend Mary Blevins, brought a family feel to the tavern when they took over in 1985, adding another must-try item to the menu: pie.

But it's not just some wimpy apple or lemon meringue pie that you find at a roadside restaurant. These are homemade chocolate cream, butterscotch, and coconut cream pies that soar a good half-foot off the plate. They are made fresh in the kitchen every day. In fact when I first saw them in the glassed-in cooler, I thought the window was distorting the size of the slices. I was wrong. They really are sky high.

As I said, it is a family kind of place. The day we stopped by, we found farmers wearing bib overalls and John Deere baseball caps sitting next to businessmen in tailored suits, while at another table a nun was chatting with several women and youngsters.

Waldo, Ohio, and fried bologna. They sort of go together.

G & R Tavern, home of the famous fried bologna sandwich.

G & R Tavern
103 N Marion St • Waldo, OH   740-726-9685
www.gandrtavern.com

Waldo is near Marion, and the area offers many other things to see and do. For ideas, contact:

Marion Area Convention and Visitors Bureau
www.visitmarionohio.com • 740-389-9770

NORTHEAST OHIO

Stan Hywet, the Gem of Akron

Akron

It sprawls across the meadow-like lawn as if it were some grand Tudor manor house in the English countryside.

Stan Hywet—the name means "stone quarry" in Old English.

A sandstone quarry was the main feature of the property when the house was built between 1912 and 1915. It was the magnificent estate of F. A. Seiberling, who with his brother Charles founded the Goodyear Tire and Rubber Company. The 65-room mansion has 23 fireplaces, and the estate today consists of five buildings and eight gardens packed into 70 acres.

In 1957, the Seiberling family donated Stan Hywet to a non-profit corporation that operates the estate and preserves it by opening the house and gardens to the public. Stan Hywet today is the sixth-largest historic home in the entire nation open to the public.

Over the years I have made several One Tank Trips to Stan Hywet, from early spring when the gardens first bloom, to cold winter nights during the holidays when the lawns, gardens, and manor house become magical with lights and music of the season.

Each Father's Day for more than 60 years, Stan Hywet has hosted a car show for lovers of classic cars. The show attracts more than 400 classic automobiles, and is one of the main car shows in northeastern Ohio.

Stan Hywet Hall has more than 60 rooms

The estate is usually closed January through March each year, but opens in the spring for their annual Easter egg hunt and breakfast for kids.

If you're curious about how the wealthy of our nation once lived, Stan Hywet is the perfect place to satisfy that curiosity. There are wonderful stories associated with every room and building on the estate. From Hollywood royalty to founding fathers of Alcoholics Anonymous, they all stayed at Stan Hywet.

One of my favorite memories of Stan Hywet occurred some years ago when Virgil Dominic was news director of Fox 8 TV in Cleveland.

He had arranged for most of the station's staff to go to the mansion to sing Christmas carols. A camera crew filmed the event, all of us gathered in the beautiful two-story-high music room and singing. That video was later shown several times on Fox 8 during the holiday season.

Whenever I think of Akron, I think of Stan Hywet.

Stan Hywet Hall and Gardens
714 North Portage Path • Akron, OH   330-836-5533
www.stanhywet.org

For other suggestions in the area, contact:

Akron Summit Convention and Visitors Bureau
www.visitakron-summit.org • 330-374-7560

Adventures on Portage Lakes

Akron

I have often thought of the Portage Lakes as one of Ohio's best-kept secrets.

They don't seem to get the attention that other waterways in the Buckeye State attract, yet they are beautiful at all times of year and offer a relaxing destination for a One Tank Trip.

First, a little history.

The lakes, both natural and man-made, sprawl over six square miles in southern Summit County. They were originally kettle lakes formed by ice during the glacial period. In modern times, the building of the Ohio-Erie Canal nearby included digging several feeder lakes or reservoirs to supply water for the canal.

Native Americans were also associated with the area because of its perfect location, where part of the lakes drain into the Tuscarawas and, eventually, the Ohio River; on the northern end, they drain toward Lake Erie. This allowed Native Americans to travel through the Ohio wilderness by water from the Ohio River to Lake Erie.

Today, Portage Lakes are used primarily for sports and recreation.

The channels between the various lakes and reservoirs are lined with beautiful homes. In the spring, summer, and fall, the lakes are alive with pontoon boats, canoes, kayaks, and fishing boats. In winter, you'll find skaters and snowmobiles darting over the smooth ice.

One of the best ways to see Portage Lakes is on a pontoon boat with **Portage Lakes Cruises**. Retired nurse Judy Narducci offers perhaps one of the best, most relaxing, most knowledgeable tours of the waterways that make up Portage Lakes. A life-long resident of the area, Judy knows the people and the history of the lakes. She has two large pontoon boats that she and her crew offer for charter each summer. You can even have dinner on board the boats as you take an evening cruise past the beautiful homes and businesses. Judy points out the best places to eat, fish, or rent a kayak or other kinds of watercraft. She can answer questions about some of the mansions along the banks of the lakes, such as the **Franklin Park Civic Center**, also known as the Tudor House.

Portage Lakes—one of Ohio's best-kept secrets. Many beautiful homes are built along the shores.

The 20-room mansion sits on almost six acres of land overlooking the lake. It was built in the 1920s by a senior executive of the B. F. Goodrich Tire Company (now Goodrich Corp.) as a wedding gift for his grandson. Today, Tudor House is owned by the Ohio Department of Natural Resources, managed by the village of Franklin, and used as the Franklin Park Civic Center.

It is rented out for weddings, parties, and other events throughout the year.

If you crave some ice cream after the boat ride, Captain Judy will undoubtedly point you toward nearby **Pav's Creamery**.

Pav's has been a favorite in the Portage Lakes area for more than half a century.

It started out in the 1950s as a Tastee Freez, but when Robert Pavlik purchased the business in the 1960s, he changed the name to "Pav's," his nickname.

Over the years, they have continued to use old-fashioned frozen custard machines such as those once used at the Euclid Beach Amusement Park in Cleveland. The slower mixing speed produces a smoother, richer flavor.

The small walk-up ice cream stand has won many awards in the last few years for "best" ice cream. Long lines of children and adults waiting for ice cream on a warm summer day seem to give credence to the awards.

Pav's Creamery
3769 Manchester Rd • Akron, OH   330-644-8524
www.pavscreamery.com

Franklin Park Civic Center – The Tudor House
655 Latham Ln • Akron, OH   330-664-1728
www.newfranklin.org

Portage Lakes Cruises, LLC
Akron, OH   330-760-0270
www.portagelakescruises.com

For more ideas in the area, see other chapters in this book or:

Akron Summit Convention and Visitors Bureau
www.visitakron-summit.org • 330-374-7560

Christ's Manger in Ohio

Akron

Springfield Township, south of Akron, might not be the place where Christ was born but it is home to one of two replicas in the United States of the tiny cave in Bethlehem where the actual birth is said to have taken place.

The other is in Washington, D.C.

The **Ohio Bethlehem Cave and Nativity Museum** is located in the basement of the Nativity of the Lord Jesus Catholic Church on Myersville Road. It was built in 1992, the idea of the pastor, Father David Halaiko, who had traveled to the Holy Land several times to visit the original site. He took measurements and photos at the Bethlehem church to make the replica as authentic as possible.

The day I visited the church, a guide pointed out that the dimensions of the man-made cave are the same as the site in Bethlehem except the cave is only half the length of the one in the Holy Land.

The main feature is the Altar of the Nativity.

On the floor, directly beneath the altar, is a large metal star, exactly like the one in Bethlehem. A hole in the center of the star contains a stone from the Cave Church at Shepherd's Fields in Bethlehem. The Latin inscription on the star translates to: "Here Jesus Christ was born of the Virgin Mary."

Across the cave is a hollowed-out section of the wall that in biblical times was used by travelers as a manger to feed their animals. The Bible says that the baby Jesus was placed in such a manger.

Against another wall is the Altar of the Magi on which you will find a small box containing frankincense and myrrh, two of the three gifts that the three kings, or wise men, brought as gifts to the newborn baby Jesus. Some gold coins were the third gift. By the way, frankincense and myrrh are simply gums and resins from trees that grow in East Africa and the Middle East. They were valued for their aromatic qualities and well as some medicinal uses.

Next to the room housing the cave is a small museum that displays hundreds of nativity scenes from countries around the world, some as tiny as a matchbox while others were crafted with whatever mate-

A replica of a manger in a cave, such as the one Christ was laid in after his birth.

rials were available, such as one carved out of a steel drum that was donated to the museum by people in Haiti.

Included in the tour is the Springfield Township church itself, built in 1992 to reflect the fourth century, A. D. church in Bethlehem. As you enter the church, you notice a row of crosses exactly 53 inches from the floor across each door reminding visitors that the original entrance to the church in the Holy Land is just 53 inches high to make it more difficult for hostile invaders to enter the church.

Tours are free, but donations are accepted. Reservations are requested for guided tours. The cave and museum are available during regular office hours at the church and before and after weekend Masses.

Ohio Bethlehem Cave and Nativity Museum
Nativity of the Lord Jesus Catholic Church
2425 Myersville Rd • Akron, OH   330-699-5086
www.nativityofthelord.org

For more ideas in this area, see other chapters in this book or:

Akron Summit Convention and Visitors Bureau
www.visitakron-summit.org • 330-374-7560

First Woman to Fly

North Canton

Ohio has rock-solid aviation credentials: the Wright Brothers, John Glenn, Neil Armstrong, and Almina Martin.

Almina Martin?

You might have never heard of Almina Martin, but she played a key role in aviation history. It happened back in 1909. Almina's husband, William Martin, cousin of fellow aviation pioneer Glen Martin, was an inventor. He had been tinkering with airplanes and had come up with a new design. Instead of two wings top and bottom, he had designed a craft that he thought could fly with just one top wing.

January 12, 1909, was a cold day. Snow covered the fields of Martin's farm in Canton. William and Almina carried his monoplane to the top of a small hill and then tied a very long rope to the front of the craft. The other end was hitched to the family horse, Old Billy, who was encouraged to start trotting across the snowy fields.

William Martin was at the controls as the craft lifted into the air to a height of about 20 feet and glided behind the galloping horse for about 200 feet before the horse slowed and the glider, with Martin aboard, came softly back to earth.

Hoping to get more altitude in the next flight, Martin exchanged seats with Almina, who weighed much less than he.

Wrapped in a long winter coat, she took the controls on the glider and as the horse galloped down the field again, she lifted off, snow falling away from the struts on the bottom of the craft. For a few brief moments, she not only soared into the winter skies, but also into the history books as the first woman to fly a heavier-than-air craft. She also became the first woman to fly a mono-wing airplane.

Many years later, Almina was asked what she remembered about that history-making flight. "It was like floating on a cloud," she said.

Martin later donated his monoplane glider to the Smithsonian Institution in Washington, D.C., where it was hung in the entrance next to Charles A. Lindbergh's *Spirit of St. Louis*.

Years later, during remodeling at the Smithsonian, it was taken down and eventually given to the William McKinley Presidential

Historic aircraft are restored and displayed at the MAPS Museum *(Military Air Preservation Society)*

Library and Museum in Canton, where it was placed into storage for several years. Finally it was loaned to the **MAPS Air Museum** at Akron-Canton Airport where it is now proudly hanging, as if in flight, in the museum hangar next to modern-day aircraft. Housed in a former National Guard hangar, there are aircraft inside and out. They even have a gondola from a Goodyear Blimp on display.

MAPS, run by the Military Air Preservation Society, is perhaps the largest aviation museum in northeastern Ohio. It is also home to a unique memorial to the Ohio servicemen who have given their lives in the Middle Eastern wars. Named "The Fallen Feather," the memorial is comprised of hand-carved wooden eagle feathers, each dedicated to a fallen service member. The feathers are made by woodcarvers from all over Ohio.

Some of the exhibits are "hands-on," and kids can climb on and touch some of the aircraft.

MAPS Air Museum
2260 International Pkwy • North Canton, OH 330-896-6332
mapsairmuseum.org

For more ideas see other chapters in this book, or:

Canton Stark County Convention & Visitors Bureau
www.visitcanton.com • 330-454-1439

The Pie Queen of Northern Ohio

Amherst

Let me admit it: I like pie.

I'll drive quite a few miles for a good piece of homemade pie.

So when National Pie Day was coming up in January a few years ago, I decided that was a good reason for a One Tank Trip to Amherst to visit a lady I've since dubbed the "Pie Queen of Northern Ohio."

Johanna Mann and her staff at **Mama Jo Homestyle Pies** make a lot of pies—as many as 20,000 in a week leading up to the holidays. They do their baking in a former Kmart converted into a huge kitchen with a smaller pie store in front. Pie-making seems run in her family. Her mother and sisters originally started a catering business, and when demand grew for their pies and baked goods, Johanna joined her brother Peter in launching Mama Jo Pies. Peter was the baker, using their mother's recipes; Johanna was experienced in the corporate world of marketing.

In one year, Johanna took the new pie company from zero to $1 million in sales. Now, years later, the business continues to grow. Peter left the company in the 1990s; Johanna heads the business.

The thousands of pies produced each day are still made mostly by hand. Johanna is getting ready to retire and is slowly turning the company over to her children: Ken Dumke, Jr., who is now general manager, and her daughter Jenna Rabosyuk, who is taking over the retail portion of the business.

The success of their pies and the reason they are in demand in a major grocery store chain is probably because they contain no preservatives: the fruit is fresh and flash frozen, and the crusts are made with a secret ingredient, lard. Yep, lard, that natural pig byproduct that your grandmother probably used not only for baking her pies, but for preparing everything from potatoes to fried chicken.

I know, I know, lard is not the healthiest thing to eat. But it tastes good and it makes the crust light and flaky, and recent studies suggest the other oils used in baking aren't significantly better than lard for your health. Like all things that taste good, eat it in moderation.

Now I thought when I visited Mama Jo that it would be interesting

The crew at Mama Jo's really knows how to make pies.

to become part of the baking crew. I kind of pictured myself up to my elbows in chocolate pudding and stirring a fresh pot of cooked apples, the air filled with the aromas from bubbling cauldrons of blueberries, raspberries, and peaches.

I saw those sights and smelled those smells not from in front of an oven, but with my hands deep in a large sink filled with dishwater, washing dirty pots and pans. It seems that is where you start if you want to be part of the baking crew.

But as the oven started discharging pie after pie, it was all worth it. There was French silk, a caramel-apple-walnut pie, apple crumb, pumpkin, Key lime. It was difficult to make a choice when it came time to purchase one to take home.

Mama Jo Pies offers many flavors, but the big sellers year-round are apple and chocolate cream. They also offer pumpkin all year. "It's not just for Thanksgiving and Christmas," Johanna notes.

Mama Jo Homestyle Pies
1969 Cooper Foster Park Rd • Amherst, OH   440-960-7437
www.mamajopies.com

For more ideas in this area, see other chapters in this book or:

The Lorain County Visitors Bureau
www.visitloraincounty.com •

Ashland, a Town of Nice People

Ashland

There is a sign on the outskirts of Ashland, put there by a realty company that proclaims: "Discover Ashland, World Headquarters of Nice People."

The town leaders have not endorsed the sign officially, but they should, because Ashland truly is a nice town, with nice people.

In fact, their university, by the same name, uses cookies to entice new students to enroll.

According to an Ashland University spokesperson, the practice started back in 1991, when enrollment in the school had dipped.

For many years, students had raved about the good food at the school and, especially the chocolate chip cookies made in the university's kitchens.

So the school started sending out a huge chocolate chip cookie to prospective students, and enrollment increased by 30 percent that year. They have been doing it every year since.

The recipe for the cookie is secret, but it produces a four-inch cookie with huge chunks of chocolate that has been a favorite with students and alumni for years.

If you would like to try the cookies, you can stop in at the university's **John C. Myers Convocation Center** and buy one in the dining area, which is open to the public.

By the way, you will also notice four-foot-tall concrete eagles all over the campus. The eagle is the school's mascot.

The eagle statues looks exactly like the eagle that is the symbol of Case Farm Tractors. This fact has not been overlooked by students, who through the years have periodically kidnapped the local Case Tractor dealer's statue and set it up somewhere on campus. The dealer would then have to haul it back to his dealership, only to probably see it disappear again when a new crop of students arrived.

Case finally donated the molds to make the concrete eagles to the university as well as a 25-foot-tall steel eagle, "Old Abe," which now stands at the center of the campus.

Which, again, proves Ashland is a town of friendly people.

It's not an official slogan, but it might as well be.

In fact, Ashland claims to have more churches than pizza restaurants or drug stores.

They also have a candy store that has been in business for more than 80 years.

The **Candy & Nut Shoppe** has been a fixture downtown since the 1930s. According to the current owner, Ray Weaver, people's tastes in candy haven't changed much over the decades.

Weaver says he has gone along with making chocolate-covered potato chips, but he has drawn the line at chocolate-covered bacon. He does think health-conscious consumers now eat more dark chocolate than in earlier years.

If you remember the smells and the taste of the old fashioned candy stores of your youth, you will feel right at home at the Candy & Nut Shoppe in Ashland.

After all those cookies and candy, you might be thinking about lunch. There is this restaurant tucked away in a strip mall on the edge of town. You can smell the barbecue as you park your car.

Welcome to **Belly Busters BBQ**.

Here, Will and Linda Anderson smoke and barbecue just about everything but the desserts. You want a smoked hot dog? They have it. They are also known for their pulled pork, hamburgers, and especially their ribs. Both the St. Louis style and baby back ribs are smoked to perfection.

And those desserts? The cakes, cookies, and brownies are made them from scratch every day.

At lunchtime, the place is usually packed with factory workers sitting next to students and office workers.

Belly Busters BBQ does a good carry-out business, as well.

John C. Myers Convocation Center
Ashland University • 401 College Ave • Ashland, OH   419-289-4142
www.ashland.edu

Candy & Nut Shoppe
39 E Main St • Ashland, OH   419-281-2766
www.facebook.com/candynutshoppe

Belly Busters BBQ
1159 E Main St • Ashland, OH   419-903-0930
www.bellybustersbbqdining.com

War Birds of Ashtabula County

Austinburg

You are driving on Ohio Route 45, just south of the community of Austinburg, when a man steps onto the highway, signaling you to stop. Suddenly, off to the left, you hear a roaring engine, and a silver airplane with World War II markings taxis across the highway into the parking lot of a factory.

Welcome to **Titan Aircraft Supply**, home of the T-51, a three-quarter-size replica of the famous P-51 Mustang fighter plane that served with distinction in WWII and Korea. The T-51 was the brain child of plane designer John Williams, who wanted to build a "kit" aircraft that would look like the famed single-seat fighter plane, but would have modern motors, carry two people, and have a range of 600 miles.

The factory, south of Austinburg, manufactures most of the parts for the aircraft, but because the T-51 is considered an amateur, home-built, experimental aircraft, the purchaser of the plane must do much of the assembly work. However, the factory works closely with purchasers to make sure they build an airplane that will fly safely. So far, says Williams, they have created over 200 of the aircraft.

Visitors are welcome at Titan Aircraft, and as you wander the large

The T-51, a three-quarter-size replica of the famous P-51, at Titan Aircraft Supply.

factory, you'll see sheet metal and framework being molded into T-51s and an Ultralite-like plane called the Tornado, which Williams also makes in kit-form.

If you're lucky, you might visit on a day that test pilot Bill Koleno takes one of the finished aircraft up for a flight from the grass strip across from the factory.

The T-51 has become a popular attraction and can be seen at many air shows in Ohio and other states.

Titan Aircraft Supply
1419 State Rte 45 • Austinburg, OH   440-275-3205
www.titanaircraft.com

For more in the area, see other chapters in this book or:

Ashtabula County Convention & Visitors Bureau
www.visitashtabulacounty.com • 440-275-3202

Covered Bridge Capital of Ohio

Ashtabula County, Jefferson

As of the writing of this book, there is a tie for the title of Ohio's Covered Bridge Capital. Both Fairfield County in Central Ohio and Ashtabula County in Northeast Ohio have 18 covered bridges. But because Ashtabula, in addition to having America's largest covered bridge also has two pizza restaurants made from an original covered bridge, I am giving the title to them.

In Europe and Asia, there have been bridges made of wood with wooden covers over the structure for many centuries. In America, the first covered bridge was built some time between 1800 and 1804 near Philadelphia, Pennsylvania. The idea spread across the northeast, then into the Great Lakes region and across the country as pioneers pushed westward.

The reason for wood bridges is obvious. On the frontier and in settlements where there was no industry, there were plenty of forests with big trees and therefore plenty of wood. The reason for covering bridges? Wooden bridges exposed to the winter and summer weather might last for about 10 years, but when covered with a roof, the heavy wooden beams that formed the bridge could last for nearly a century.

Beginning in 1867, shortly after the Civil War, there was a building boom in Ashtabula County, and many bridges built then are still in existence. Today, there are 18 covered bridges scattered across Ashtabula County, the largest county in the state and, fittingly, home of the largest covered bridge in the United States.

At 613 feet long, the **Smolen-Gulf Bridge** carries traffic across the Ashtabula River near the Plymouth and Ashtabula Township line. The bridge was named in honor of long-time Ashtabula County Engineer John Smolen, who championed replacing some steel bridges with new covered bridges because the wooden ones lasted longer and were a better investment. In addition, the bridges become tourist attractions that brought money to the community.

Interestingly, after winning the title for the longest covered bridge in the United States, the county earned the distinction of also having the shortest covered bridge in the nation.

The Smolen-Gulf Bridge in Ashtabula County. *(Visit Ashtabula County)*

On West Liberty Street in Geneva, you will find a covered bridge just 18 feet long. This one just carries traffic over a wide ditch. Again, a covered bridge was chosen because it was less expensive than replacing the large culvert that originally allowed traffic to pass over the stream. It, too, was designed by County Engineer John Smolen.

For years, the title for the longest covered bridge in the state was held by the **Harpersfield Bridge** near Geneva. The 228-foot-long span, built in 1868, crosses the Grand River. Its unusual design, half covered bridge and half steel bridge, was brought about by a flood in 1913 that took out the north end of the river bank and widened the river channel. A steel bridge was constructed to attach the covered bridge to the northern shore. Today, it is perhaps the most accessible of all the bridges, and a park has been developed on both sides of the river so picnics can be held with the bridge in the background.

Ashtabula County residents celebrate their bridges and their heritage each autumn with the Ashtabula County Covered Bridge Festival, which is held at the county fairgrounds in Jefferson on the second weekend in October. There is a parade, a farmers' market, quilt shows, music, food, and lots of fun and entertainment.

Any time of year is a great time to take a driving tour of the many bridges in the county. You can get a detailed map showing how to find each bridge location from the festival headquarters in Jefferson.

Whenever I take a One Tank Trip to Ashtabula County, I always try to build in time to stop for lunch at the **Jefferson Diner** in Jefferson.

A classic diner in Jefferson, located in a World War II quonset hut. *(OZinOH)*

The diner is located in a historic World War II quonset hut directly across from the county court house. Owners Gary and Anita Licate have created a diner that I wish all other diners would copy.

Anita bakes pies every day that have won awards at the county fair. The Licates make their food from scratch in the kitchen, using very little processed and frozen ingredients.

The fare is simple and pretty much what you would expect to find at a diner: spaghetti and meatballs, creamed chicken over biscuits, and the diner's famous "Wimpy burger" that requires using two hands to eat.

Covered Bridge Festival
25 W Jefferson St • Jefferson, OH   440-576-3769
www.coveredbridgefestival.org

Jefferson Diner
20 N Chestnut St • Jefferson, OH   440-576-1977

For more in Ashtabula County, see other chapters in this book or:

Ashtabula Convention & Visitors Bureau
www.visitashtabulacounty.com • 440-275-3202

Football and Other Canton Traditions

Canton

We all know that professional football was born in Canton, Ohio. It's a city not only rich in sports history, but also in politics—and it has some interesting places to eat, too.

When I take one of my favorite One Tank Trips to Canton to visit the Pro Football Hall of Fame and to stop at two of my favorite eating places, **Taggart's Ice Cream Parlor** and Kennedy Barbecue Inc., I am reminded of a line from the play *Fiddler on the Roof*: "It's tradition!"

Taggart's first opened its doors in 1922, the same year the professional football team owners gathered in this Ohio town to form what became the NFL. Legend has it that football immortal Jim Thorpe, who played for the Canton Bulldogs, enjoyed the homemade ice cream at Taggart's while sitting in the same wooden booths that have been in the building for nearly 100 years.

It is a well-established fact that founder of the American Football League, Lamar Hunt, would treat each year's class of inductees to the hall of fame to Taggart's house specialty, The "Bittner," named for a long-ago local baseball team that wanted a really thick ice cream drink. The Bittner is a sort-of milkshake made with three-quarters of a pound of homemade vanilla ice cream topped with Taggart's own chocolate sauce and beaten until it reaches liquid consistency. Then a handful of freshly roasted pecans are added to the mixture, and the whole thing is capped with whipped cream and a cherry.

Some Hall of Fame members, such as Bob St. Clair of the San Francisco Giants and sports broadcaster Dan Dierdorf, have been regular customers whenever they visited Canton.

It is much the same story at another Canton Landmark, **Kennedy Barbecue**, a tiny restaurant on Fourth Street across from Monumental Park. Opened in the early 1920s, Kennedy also has hosted Lamar Hunt as well as a more infamous hall of famer, O.J. Simpson. The restaurant can seat about 35 people at the counter, table and booths.

The big attraction at Kennedy's is the smoked meat and their homemade relish.

The "Bittner" a ¾-pound ice cream specialty that has been served at Taggarts' Ice Cream Parlour since the 1920s.

There is a small smokehouse behind the kitchen where hams, turkeys and pork roasts are smoked and slow cooked daily. The menu is simple: sliced smoked ham, pork, beef, or turkey sandwiches topped with "Jack Kennedy's relish." The relish is made from a secret recipe that includes finely ground cabbage, mustard, and peppers.

The two soups on the menu are the homemade bean soup or chili; the desserts are Amish-made pies and ice cream.

Long-time owner Jack Kennedy passed away in June 2009, and his family kept the business going after his death, but finally decided that perhaps it was time to close.

Ernie Schott, who owns Taggart's and was a long-time friend of Kennedy's, decided the barbecue restaurant was a bit of Canton history and should not fade away, so he and his wife Patti purchased the diminutive restaurant and vowed to keep it going "just like it was."

They did make some changes. After a couple of break-ins, Kennedy had replaced two large front windows with sheets of plywood. Schott took down the plywood and replaced it with new windows. He also kept the name and painted the place inside and out, making it brighter and more appealing.

Despite the small size of the establishment, Kennedy's does a large carry-out business in sandwiches and whole smoked hams and roasts for parties.

But the main fun is stopping in after a Hall of Fame ceremony. You never know whether you might be seated next to an NFL great, sharing some Kennedy Barbecue.

Of course, one of the chief reasons to travel to Canton is to stop at the **Pro Football Hall of Fame**, now more than a half-century old. It attracts upwards of three-quarters of a million visitors each year who come to gaze on the memorabilia and busts of football greats.

In 1963, when the hall was built, the entire museum and complex fitted into just 19,000 square feet. It is dwarfed by today's giant hall and museum that encompass almost 120,000 square feet.

The NFL Hall of Fame is constantly evolving, adding to the theaters, enshrinee memorabilia, gift shop, and everything football.

Even if you are not a football fan, you are bound to find something of interest when you visit this popular attraction.

Like I said, "It's tradition."

Taggart's Ice Cream Parlor
1401 Fulton Rd NW • Canton, OH   330-452-6844
www.taggartsicecream.com

Kennedy Barbecue Inc.
1420 7th St NW • Canton, OH   330-454-0193
www.taggartsicecream.com/Kennedy_Barbeque.html

The Pro Football Hall of Fame
2121 George Halas Dr • Canton, OH   330-456-8207
www.profootballhof.com

Cars I Have Loved

Canton

Everyone who has ever watched One Tank Trips knows that I like cars. No. I LOVE cars. Probably the most asked question I've gotten from viewers over the years is about one car: my 1959 Nash Metropolitan convertible. I still own the car. It's on long-term loan to the Canton Classic Car Museum.

Shortly after One Tank Trips began in 1980 on WJW TV, I decided I needed a symbol for my travel reports. It made sense to find a car that people would quickly associate with me and remind them to tune in to Channel 8 to see what I was up to.

The first car I thought of was a Bantam American. I had had one in high school. The diminutive car filled the bill several ways. It was made in America, in Butler, Pennsylvania. It was small and looked cute. And it would be cheap to operate. However, when I suggested that the television station buy the car so it could be used as a traveling billboard, my boss, Virgil Dominic, said no.

So I set off to see if I could borrow one. Finally, friends Bill and Bonnie Cutcher of Vermilion came to my rescue. Bill was a big car collector and owned the 1946 Chevrolet convertible that we had used in early shows. He came up with a 1940 Bantam convertible, which was perfect. The problem was, we just used the car once or twice a year to shoot opens, and after a while, people began to expect to see me driving the little Bantam everywhere. They would be disappointed when we'd pull up in a late-model news cruiser.

As One Tank Trips gained more popularity, we got more inquiries about my "little red car," which I didn't own. I decided something had to be done. Trying again to get the television station to buy some kind of small car for me failed, so I talked with my wife Bonnie, and we decided to buy it ourselves.

I recalled from my youth the popularity of the tiny Nash Metropolitan. Designed in Italy, partly assembled by a British auto manufacturer, and with final assembly in the United States, it was a truly international car. Sadly, the company had stopped making it in 1962. So I launched a hunt for an existing model. I found it in a car collec-

A 1937 Studebaker at the Canton Classic Car Museum. It's believed to be the longest-serving police car in U.S. history.

tor's warehouse in North Canton. After some negotiation, I became its owner.

For the next dozen or so years, the little red-and-white Nash Metropolitan was my companion in all my stories. Over the years, we appeared in parades. We even were invited to be the first automobile to make the ceremonial first drive across the reconstructed Shoreway Bridge in downtown Cleveland. When I retired (the first time), in 2004, the **Canton Classic Car Museum** asked to display the car. It seemed appropriate that the car should return to its home county. I agreed, and it has been there ever since.

The museum also has a 1957 BMW Isetta, a tiny car with only one door that I drove for about a year and a half on the show. That car was not made for modern highways, and I donated it to the museum.

Every car in the museum has a story to tell. For instance they have America's longest-serving police car. It all began during the Great Depression, when the city of Canton decided to purchase not just a new police vehicle, but an armored one.

Depending on the version you hear, the need for a bullet-proof car was brought about by either Canton's reputation as "Little Chicago," with lots of gangsters passing through or making their headquarters here, or that an understaffed police force needed the armored automobile to deal with the violence associated with the labor movement in the 1930s.

Whatever the reason, the city purchased the car in 1937 for $800, a nominal price for a new car at the time, and immediately spent an additional $4,600 for armor protection, which added 3,000 pounds of 10-gauge steel plating, replacing windows with 1⅛-inch-thick bullet-resistant glass that included portholes so the officers could shoot safely at desperados and criminals from inside the tank-like car. They even wrapped the gasoline tank in a steel cocoon and replaced the wheels with double walled tires that could not be easily flattened by bullets.

But in their haste to make the car bullet-proof, the designers forgot to include anything for the comfort of the officers who had to drive the auto. According to Char Lautzenheiser of the Canton Classic Car Museum, the car had no ventilation. "Just imagine," she said, "in those days before air conditioning, sitting in a black car, wearing wool uniforms in an Ohio summer, and not being able to lower the windows more than three inches. The only relief was two small fans that were installed as an afterthought."

For most of its career, the car, which local police dubbed "The Flying Squadron," was used to transfer large sums of money between businesses in Canton. But in 1958, it proved its worth in dramatic fashion.

Two armed and dangerous robbers had holed up in a farmhouse near Louisville, Ohio, and were holding an entire family hostage. The standoff between the crooks and the local sheriff's department had gone on for more than a day when the exasperated sheriff put in a call to Canton for "The Flying Squadron." According to printed reports of that day, the big, black armored car came roaring down the driveway through a hail of bullets, pulled up in front of a window in the house, and police inside the car fired tear-gas through the portholes into the home. Within moments, the robbers had surrendered and the family was safe.

The armored car continued to serve Canton until 1996, when it was retired and donated to the Canton Classic Car Museum. By that time, it had been on active duty for a total of 59 years, making it perhaps the longest serving police car in America.

Canton Classic Car Museum
123 Sixth St SW • Canton, OH   330-455-3603
www.cantonclassiccar.org

Some Presidential Trivia

I have always been fascinated by presidential lore, and Ohio is rich in presidents who were either born here or got their start in the Buckeye State. I thought it might be fun to look at some trivia about Ohio's many connections to the U.S. presidency and suggest a series of One Tank Trips to some of the Buckeye State's presidential sites.

Did you know that Ohio-born Ulysses S. Grant's birthplace in Point Pleasant was once placed on a barge and floated up and down the Mississippi River by a promoter?

Or that, while in office, Marion resident Warren G. Harding had a pet dog, Laddie Boy, who became so popular that a garden club in Marion commissioned a stained glass window depicting the dog, and children across the country donated money to build a statue of Laddie Boy?

That Rutherford B. Hayes, of Fremont, is buried next to Old Whitey, the horse he rode in the Civil War, or that the gates to the Hayes estate in Fremont, Spiegel Grove, once guarded the White House?

That Lyndon Johnson was sworn in as president aboard Air Force One and that historic craft now makes its home in Dayton as part of the presidential aircraft collection at the National Museum of the United States Air Force?

Did you know that only one of our dead presidents was never really buried? James Garfield's flag-draped casket still can be seen as he lies in state in a basement vault at the Garfield Memorial in Cleveland's Lake View Cemetery.

For sheer numbers of presidential sites and artifacts, the title probably goes to the city of Canton.

Standing tall on the skyline of the city is the imposing tomb of our 25th president, William McKinley. You can also visit Saxton House, once home to William and Ida McKinley and now part of the **National First Ladies Library and Museum**, located at 331 South Market Avenue.

The McKinley Administration also had its scandals. One happened at 319 Lincoln Avenue in Canton, where George Saxton, brother of the president's wife, Ida, was shot while he was leaving the home of a

The magnificent tomb of President William McKinley in Canton.

widowed friend. A former girlfriend was arrested, tried, and acquitted. The case was never solved.

The church where McKinley taught Sunday school and where his funeral services were held is open to the public. Church of the Savior Methodist Church is located at 120 Cleveland Avenue, S.W.

Owned by relatives of President McKinley, the Canton Classic Car Museum mixes old cars, nostalgia, and McKinley memorabilia. It's at Market Avenue S.W. and Sixth Street.

At the **William McKinley Presidential Library and Museum**, you can be greeted by, and listen to, life-size, animatronic William and Ida McKinley as they discuss his presidency. The museum has the largest collection of McKinley memorabilia in the country. It also contains exhibits honoring other early Canton achievers such as H. Earl Hoover, Henry Timken, and Charles Diebold. There is a street with reproductions of early local stores and businesses and a wonderful model train display for re-living Stark County history.

Among many other interesting displays is the unusual two-sided desk that President McKinley used in the White House. He sat on one side and his secretary, George Cortelyou, sat on the opposite.

George Washington might be on the $1 bill, but did you know that McKinley's portrait graced the $500 bill, and that the red carnation that is the state flower of Ohio was McKinley's favorite flower? According to curator Kimberly Kenney, there is some evidence that McKinley really favored pink carnations, and it was only after his assassination that the red carnation was preferred.

McKinley was the last of our presidents to have served in the Civil War. While serving in the army as a commissary sergeant, he was commended for bringing hot coffee to troops under fire. The Library and Museum now sells packages of "Coffee Bill Hero's Blend" coffee featuring a photo of Sgt. Bill McKinley as souvenirs.

There is a final bit of trivia about McKinley: He was the first president to ride in an automobile. It sadly turned out to be his first and last ride in a motorcar. The vehicle was an electric ambulance that carried him to a doctor after he was shot while greeting people at the Pan American Exposition in Buffalo, New York, in 1901. He died a few days later from the wounds.

William McKinley Presidential Library and Museum
800 McKinley Monument Dr NW • Canton, OH   330-456-7043
www.mckinleymuseum.org

National First Ladies' Library / The Ida Saxton McKinley Home
331 S. Market Ave. • Canton, OH   330-452-0876

There is much more presidential trivia to be found in Canton, such as the National First Ladies Library and Museum and many places where presidents spent the night. For more ideas, see:

Stark County Convention & Visitors Bureau
www.visitcanton.com • 330-454-1439

Some Cleveland Favorites

Cleveland

To be sure, there is much to see and do in Cleveland: the Rock N Roll Hall of Fame, the Indians, the Browns, the Cavaliers, the West Side Market.

You get the idea.

But let me suggest a few other places in town that sometimes get overlooked, especially on a bad, rainy, or snowy day.

The **Western Reserve Historical Society** is the largest privately supported regional history organization in the country. If you live in Northeast Ohio, chances are you'll find some of our collective past stored here, from the huge caricature sign of Chief Wahoo that used to grace the old Cleveland Lakefront Stadium, to the diminutive sailboat *Tinkerbelle* that once crossed the Atlantic Ocean, to one of the finest genealogy libraries in America. All this and more is stored in several buildings at University Circle. Exhibits are constantly changing, and you can have the fun of discovery just about any time of year.

But my favorite spot at the complex is the Crawford Auto and Aviation Museum, which offers nearly 200 classic and special-interest automobiles and airplanes, from one of the earliest automobiles to Bobby Rahal's 1982 March Indy car that won the first Cleveland 500 race. Did you know that in the early days of automotive history, more than 80 different cars were built in Cleveland? Learn about this and much more as you wander the floors of the museum.

Did you know that there is a museum dedicated to the role of women in air and space on Cleveland's lakefront?

The **International Women's Air and Space Museum** is located in the lobby of the Burke Lakefront Airport terminal. One of the exhibits explores the Mercury 13, the story of 13 women who were secretly trained for the Mercury space program in the 1960s.

The museum began in 1986 in Centerville, Ohio, a Dayton suburb, but soon outgrew its quarters. In 1998, it moved to Cleveland.

Exhibits commemorate such women as Jacqueline Cochran, the first woman to fly faster than sound, and Valentina Tereshkova of the Soviet Union, who became the first woman to orbit the Earth. There

The Crawford Auto-Aviation Museum has one of the best auto collections in Ohio *(Western Reserve Historical Society)*

are also tributes to the women who flew in World War II and aviation pioneers Amelia Earhart, Ruth Nichols, and others.

The museum exhibits are open seven days a week. Admission is free.

If the names Frankie Yankovic or Johnny Vadnal are familiar to you, you are probably a fan of Cleveland-style polka music. The **National Cleveland-Style Polka Hall of Fame and Museum** is located in Euclid.

Here you will see Johnny Pecon's accordion and the costumes worn on stage by polka-great Frankie Yankovic.

Cleveland-style polka music is different from traditional polkas, according to the museum staff. In the early 1900s, Cleveland was a melting pot of European immigrants who brought their culture and music to the city. Over time, the musical traditions blended and evolved into a unique style.

The hall of fame includes not only the many inductees and their instruments, but also videos of great performances. There is also a museum store where you can purchase CDs and videos of Cleveland-style polka performers. The museum and store are open Tuesday through Saturday.

Kids and adults will find a visit to the **Cleveland Police Museum** interesting. Tucked away on the first floor of the Justice Center, the museum offers a look at Cleveland police history, complete with life-size exhibits including the Untouchables' Eliot Ness and the department's nationally known mounted unit.

There is even a bit of the macabre in the exhibit about the Kingsbury Run murders of the 1930s, such as plaster of paris life masks used by the coroner's office to identify some of the victims. There is also a booking area and a jail cell, where kids can pose for pictures.

The museum is open Monday through Friday, and admission is free.

The Western Reserve Historical Society
10825 East Blvd • Cleveland, OH   216-721-5722
www.wrhs.org

International Women's Air and Space Museum
Burke Lakefront Airport
1501 N. Marginal Rd • Cleveland, OH   216-623-1111
www.iwasm.org

National Cleveland Style Polka Hall of Fame and Museum
605 E 222nd St • Euclid, OH   216-261-3263
www.clevelandstyle.com

Cleveland Police Museum
1300 Ontario St • Cleveland, OH   216-623-5055
www.clevelandpolicemuseum.org

There is much more to see and do in Cleveland. For ideas, see:

Destination Cleveland
www.thisiscleveland.com   216-875-6600

White Turkey Drive-In

Conneaut

One of the things I have learned from the years I have been on the road searching for new destinations is, we all love the unusual. I found just such a place in Conneaut, Ohio: the **White Turkey Drive-In**. Drive-in restaurants usually specialize in hamburgers, french fries, and milk-shakes. Not so at the White Turkey.

The restaurant was founded in 1952 when Marge and Eddie Tuttle were on vacation and stopped at a Richardson Root Beer stand. Richardson was a very popular brand at that time, and the root beer was dispensed from a huge container shaped like a wooden barrel into large glass mugs that had been stored in a freezer. Customers received the drink with foam running down the sides of a frosty glass mug.

When they returned home, the Tuttles decided to buy a Richardson franchise, but they wanted something on the menu other than hamburgers and hot dogs. At the time, they had a turkey farm and wanted to promote their White Holland turkeys, so they decided to specialize in turkey sandwiches.

Flash forward almost 65 years, and the little drive-in restaurant is still there, unchanged, on East Main Street in Conneaut.

It is all open; there are no windows. Customers sit outside on high stools at a counter wrapped around three sides of the restaurant. On the front counter sits the huge barrel that proclaims they sell Richardson Root Beer. Servers and customers alike put up with the weather, heat, and rain. When the wind blows rain under the eaves, customers move to the other side. If it's storming, the staff might drop the shutters on the side where the wind is blowing.

Although this design was common when the restaurant was built in the early 1950s, it has pretty much disappeared, and the White Turkey Drive-In is now truly one-of-a-kind.

It's the charm of this open-air drive-in and the food, especially the food, that bring the customers back each summer, year after year, generation after generation. Gary Tuttle and his wife, Peggy, took over the restaurant from his parents in 1981. When Gary passed away in 2012, his daughter Kelly Vito and her husband Bradd joined Peggy

White Turkey Drive-In, one of the last open-air drive-in restaurants.

and became the third generation of the Tuttle family to operate the iconic drive-in.

I asked Peggy Tuttle why the restaurant had not evolved like other drive-ins. She quoted her father-in-law, Eddie Tuttle: "If it ain't broke, don't fix it. People like it just the way it is."

They still serve the frosted glasses of root beer. The shredded white turkey, made with the family's special seasoning, is still the best selling sandwich. And, yes, you can get most of the things you find at other drive-ins—hot dogs, hamburgers, french fries, and milkshakes.

When you sit at the counter and order a "Large Marge"—a turkey sandwich with cheese and bacon—and a root beer float, you realize that everyone, servers and customer, seem to know each other. Chances are the server's parents or grandparents also spent their high school days as customers or employees. It's that kind of place.

Opens in early May and closes on Labor Day.

White Turkey Drive-In
388 E Main Rd • Conneaut, OH   440-593-2209
www.whiteturkey.com

For more ideas in this area, see other chapters of this book or:

Ashtabula County Convention & Visitors Bureau
www.visitashtabulacounty.com • 440-275-3202

Dover's Do-It-Yourself Museums

Dover

Dover, in Tuscarawas County, is a city rich in local and state history. You'll find everything from the state's oldest continuously operating drive-in movie theater to the home of Ohio's master carver. Visit a museum here that traces the history of commercial radio and television or go to see one of the most unusual collections of funeral memorabilia. And all of these attractions are privately owned or family-owned.

Warther Museum & Gardens in Dover is perhaps the town's best-known attraction. Thousands of school-children and adults have come away from a visit here with a pair of working wooden pliers carved from a single piece of wood in only seconds.

The museum celebrates the life of Ohio's master carver Ernest "Mooney" Warther. A man with only a second-grade education, Warther taught himself to carve. His first project used soup bones to create a model of an entire steel factory where he worked.

Later, turning to ivory and precious woods, he started to carve models representing the history of steam engines.

Over the course of a lifetime, Warther created 64 model locomotives, each tiny piece hand-carved down to the last rivet. Although he had no formal training, his works were perfectly scaled models. One of his masterpieces is a model of Lincoln's funeral train carved entirely from ivory.

To support his craft, Warther started producing knives for sale to the public. He died at the age of 87 in 1973. His family continues the knife-making business in a factory in the basement of the museum.

Tours of the museum include audio-visual presentations, displays of Warther's carvings, including his locomotives, and a visit to the knife factory to see how they are made. There is much more to see here, including gardens and collections of buttons and arrowheads.

Dover is also home to the John Herzig Funeral Memorabilia Collection.

Fittingly, the exhibit is part of the **Famous Endings Museum**, located in the Toland-Herzig Funeral Home. John Herzig tells me that it

Vintage broadcasting equipment on display at the Auman Museum of Radio & TV.

started out as an autograph collection. His first find was an autograph from former heavyweight champion Joe Louis. Its previous owner included a copy of the program from Louis's funeral in 1981.

Today, Herzig has more than 1,000 pieces of funeral memorabilia, much of it on display at his funeral home in downtown Dover.

Included in the collection is the accordion believed to have been played by U.S. Coast Guard Chief Petty Officer Graham Jackson in the iconic photograph of the funeral of President Franklin Delano Roosevelt in 1945.

Also in the collection is the original paperwork for the funeral of Gladys Presley, Elvis Presley's mother; the visitation log from the funeral of former New York Yankees manager Casey Stengel; as well as mourning vests worn by officials at the funeral of former President William McKinley. The collection is open to the public during business hours at the funeral home.

The **Lynn Auto Drive-In Theatre** in nearby Strasburg is Ohio's oldest continuously operating drive-in theater. Opened in 1937, it's the nation's second oldest drive-in. (The oldest is a drive-in movie theater near Bethlehem, Pennsylvania that opened in 1934.)

The Lynn was named for the daughter of one of the owners of the theater. Current owners Rich and Jamie Reding are the fourth generation of their family to operate the Lynn. Today the theater has two screens instead of one wireless HD sound system, but it is still one of the few "grass" theaters left in the world, a bit of movie history right here in the Buckeye State.

If you remember when a massive cabinet held a tiny seven-inch television screen, or when radio speakers were giant, curved pipes sticking out of the top of the set, take time to visit the **Auman Museum of Radio & TV** in downtown Dover.

There are over 1,000 early radio and television sets on display. Many are in working order and play taped programs from the past.

You can see the original weather boards used by Fox 8 TV meteorologist Dick Goddard, posters from the *The Gene Carroll Show* on WEWS, and even a model of the first television set used in the White House.

The museum is open by appointment only.

Warther Museum & Gardens
331 Karl Ave • Dover, OH   330-343-7513
www.warthers.com

Famous Endings Museum
Toland-Herzig Funeral Home
803 N Wooster Ave • Dover, OH   330-343-6132
www.tolandherzig.com

Lynn Auto Drive-In Theatre
9735 State Rte 250 NW • Strasburg, OH   330-878-5797
www.lynndrivein.com

Auman Museum of Radio & TV
215 Tuscarawas Ave • Dover, OH   330-364-1058
www.aumantvmuseum.com

One of the works of the "Master Carver" at Warther Carving Museum.

Ohio's Darkest Spot

Montville

I have maintained for many years that Ohio has some of the finest county-owned parks in America. Throughout this book, you will see examples of what I am talking about. But one of the most unusual is located in Geauga County. Its claim to fame is that it offers one of the darkest spots in Ohio for looking at the stars.

When was the last time you looked up on a clear night and really saw the Milky Way? **Observatory Park**, in the Geauga Park District, is one of only 15 places in America that has been deemed an optimal spot for star gazing.

The designation was made by the International Dark Sky Association, and recognizes that this 1,100-acre park in Montville Township in northern Geauga County is secluded and far enough away from city light that star gazing is possible for both amateurs and professional astronomers. Only two other parks east of the Mississippi have earned this designation.

And it's not just stars. During the daytime on the spacious grounds of the observatory area is a one-mile planetary trail, which allows a visitor to take an imaginary stroll across the solar system with rocks of various sizes representing familiar planets like the moon. Each of the eight planetary stations are in a miniature scale to show their size in the universe and there are informational plaques at each stop.

On sunny days, don't miss the giant working sundial located just off the main parking lot. It's a great place to take a family photo.

There is also a seismography station that works around the clock where you can see disturbances in the earth's surface as they happen, and the meteorology (weather) station, allows visitors to check the current barometric pressure and wind speed.

Inside the Robert McCullough Science Center, named for a long-serving park commissioner, there is a planetarium where staff members can point out stars and highlights of the galaxy, regardless of the weather or cloud cover.

But while there is much to do in the daytime, it is when darkness falls on a clear night that this park really comes to life.

A huge sun dial guards the entrance to Observatory Park, one of only 15 places in America to be deemed an optimal spot for star gazing.

Unlike many parks that close their gates at dark, Observatory Park is open most months of the year until 11:00 p.m. and in the summer, until 1:00 a.m. to accommodate star watching.

There are usually programs held on nights when something unusual is happening in the night sky. The park usually has one or more telescopes set up to give visitors a closer look at the heavens, or you can bring your own.

Right now the park's main telescope is a sophisticated reflector scope with a 25-inch mirror. It was built by astronomer Norman Oberle and donated to the park by his family.

During special programs, when the roof to the observatory is opened and the telescope is aimed at the sky, visitors can climb a ladder to peer into the giant viewfinder for a view of the stars that is simply incredible.

Observatory Park
10610 Clay St • Montville, OH   440-279-9516
www.geaugaparkdistrict.org

For other ideas, including places to dine and stay, contact:

Destination Geauga
www.destinationgeauga.com • 800-775-1538

Geneva-on-the-Lake

Geneva, Geneva-on-the-Lake

The granddaddy of all Lake Erie summer resorts is located in Ashtabula County.

It was just after the American Civil War, and veterans and their families were looking for a place with sun, beaches, water, and fishing to spend some quiet time in the summer.

That year was 1869, and war-weary families discovered a quiet picnic grove on a bluff overlooking Lake Erie. They called it Sturgeon Point because of the enormous five- to six-foot-long sturgeon that once could be fished from the lake.

Today, Geneva-on-the-Lake, so-named to differentiate it from the town of Geneva, just four miles south, is an eclectic collection of past, present, and future. The "strip" in the downtown area is little changed from the early 1950s.

On warm summer nights, it still resembles a street carnival, with its arcade lights, sounds, and smells.

They love miniature golf here. The town has several courses; the oldest miniature golf course in continuous operation in the U.S. is downtown.

Geneva State Park.

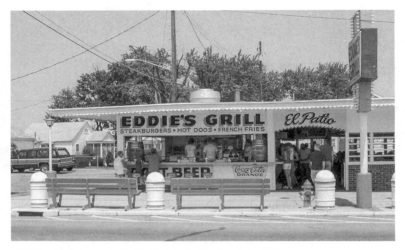

Eddie's Grill looks much like it did during its heydey in the 1950s.

Sidewalk eateries still raise their shutters to reveal counters that serve customers right on the street. **Eddie's Grill** continues to serve his popular deep-fried foot-long hot dogs. Incidentally the original "Sturgeon Point" was located right behind the building that houses Eddie's Grill.

Madsen Donuts, in business since the 1930s, finds lines of people waiting for hot donuts when they open each day throughout the summer.

The old and the new mix at the edge of the village, where Adventure Zone now stands. The merry-go-round that operated in Erieview Park for many years has found a new home here, along with new go-kart tracks, bumper boats, batting cages, miniature golf, and a climbing wall.

My one complaint with this resort is that the summer season is very short. Many of the businesses do not open until mid-June and close by the end of August. Fortunately, there are some year-round businesses.

Farther to the west is the Geneva State Park, which has a new bike trail that runs through the park to the village. Along the trail, you pass a 300-foot-long sandy beach where sunbathers and swimmers gather.

The relatively new Resort and Conference Center, with its four-story lobby and 109 guest rooms, dominates the lakefront. It is one of only two state park lodges that offers views of the lake. The nearby marina, also part of the park, offers not only boat dockage, but is a center for the charter boat fishing industry here.

The **Old Firehouse Winery** might be the most unique attraction of all.

Located in the town's first fire station, the winery and restaurant sits at the edge of the lake and boasts a 45-foot-tall Ferris wheel offering a very different view of our world-class Lake Erie sunsets. It operates nightly throughout the summer season.

The most popular time is just before sundown, when most of the 12 seats are filled with visitors hoping to watch the sun disappear into Lake Erie. The setting is so romantic that couples getting married at the winery have made a ride on the Ferris wheel part of the ceremony.

The Old Firehouse Winery, open year-round, is home to a collection of fire department memorabilia that includes toy fire trucks, patches from various fire departments, and firefighting equipment, all displayed on the walls and suspended from the ceiling over diners in the restaurant. One of the specialties of the house is chicken marinated in Firehouse Wine and spices. In the summer, the restaurant is also known for ribs cooked on outdoor grills in a courtyard near the Ferris wheel.

The Old Firehouse Winery
5499 Lake Rd • Geneva, OH   440-466-9300
www.oldfirehousewinery.com

Eddie's Grill and Dairy Queen
5377 Lake Rd. • Geneva-on-the-Lake, OH   440-466-8720

Geneva-on-the-Lake Convention & Visitors Bureau
www.visitgenevaonthelake.com • 800-862-9948

One of the Best Places in the World for Autumn Color

Holmes County, Millersburg

In 2014 the National Geographic Society finally got around to agreeing with what I have been saying for years: that Holmes County is one of the best places to see autumn color.

That year, National Geographic Society published its list of the top 10 places in the world for fall color: Sonoma County, California; Northern New Mexico; Gaspé Peninsula, Quebec, Canada; Douro Valley, Portugal; Bavaria, Germany; Transylvania, Romania; Moscow, Russia; Jiuzhaigou Valley, Sichuan Province, China; and Kyoto, Japan.

Holmes County, Ohio, ranked number three on the list.

Amish country photographer and long-time friend Doyle Yoder isn't in the least surprised. His photos showing the beauty of the region have appeared on the covers of many national magazines and publications. He explains, "It's a combination of the simple ways of the Amish coupled with the natural beauty of the rolling hills here in Holmes County that come together in a very special way."

Starting in late September, you can find great fall foliage in not only Holmes County, but also in the surrounding counties of Coshocton, Wayne, Stark, Tuscarawas and Ashland.

When you go leaf hunting in the fall, you get a bonus by heading for Ohio's Amish country: great food, bakery, and roadside stands. There is no better way to appreciate autumn in Ohio than spending the night in the country so you can see the colors change at sunset and the dawn.

Just make your reservations early, now that the area is gaining international recognition for its beauty.

If I were making a top-10 list of One Tank Trips any time of year, Holmes County would certainly be on that list.

Holmes County Chamber of Commerce and Tourism Bureau
6 W Jackson St • Millersburg, OH   330-674-3975
www.visitamishcountry.com

A Hardware Store for the Ages

Kidron

Every man loves an old fashioned hardware store. It's like a toy store for adults.

There is a store in Kidron, near Wooster, that bills itself as "a low-tech superstore." **Lehman's Hardware and Appliances** takes pride in selling very few items that run on electricity.

Kidron is heavily populated by Mennonite and Amish families.

Back in 1955, local businessman Jay Lehman decided to start a small hardware that would cater to the needs of Amish families who, for religious reasons, still use much of the technology of the nineteenth century. Wood-burning stoves, oil-burning lamps and simple, hand-operated tools and appliances.

The business was successful but little-known outside the Amish community until the international oil crisis of 1973.

With oil and gasoline suddenly in short supply, people started looking for alternative, fuel-saving ways to live, and they discovered Lehman's Hardware.

Over the years, Lehman's has continued to grow, spurred by the Y2K controversy, when much of the world thought computers would crash when 1999 became 2000. In addition, with the tragedy of 9/11, more and more people, not just in Ohio, but across the country, discovered the simple tools and furnishings of the past still had a place in the modern world.

Today, Lehman's is a major tourist destination in Wayne County, attracting people from around the world. The simple hardware store has grown into a huge structure that nearly fills an entire city block in this small village, but the emphasis is still on low-tech.

Glenda Lehman Ervin, Jay Lehman's daughter, took me on a tour of the store and pointed out some unique items.

She said, "People are looking for authentic, practical products that also help save the environment as well as save them money."

For example, she pointed out attractive welcome mats made from recycled automobile tires. Locally produced Amish rag rugs are created from old denim jeans and work shirts. Lehman's also carries

Lehman's—like a general store from the old days, only bigger.

exotic items, such as a "peanut butter mixer," a device that attaches to a peanut butter jar and mixes the oil into the mixture without spilling it all over the counter. Some of the practical items are pretty unusual, such as the steel bar of soap, a stainless steel bar that you rub on your hands under running water like a bar of soap. The claim is that it will remove odors such as fresh-cut onions from your hands.

When it comes to toys, you won't find any computer games or Game Boys. These are the toys of a century ago, from real Flexible Flyer sleds to toboggans, gravity operated marble games, all kinds of puzzles, and hand-made wooden toys.

Glenda Ervin said, "A jump-rope, a set of dominos, or a board game, don't need batteries on Christmas morning. They're ready to use."

Since they also deal with customers in third-world countries where little electricity is available, Lehman's also sells gas- or kerosene-powered refrigerators and freezers and hand-operated washing machines, which can be ideal for people who own vacation cabins in remote areas.

Lehman's even offers some rather exotic items like soap made from donkeys' milk, which, they claim, softens the skin because of its natural ingredients: beeswax, fruit and, yes, donkeys' milk.

On the other hand if you don't like smelling like fruit or flowers after you bathe, they also sell what our ancestors used: grandma's lye soap. It doesn't smell like, well, anything. They say grandma used this soap to wash clothes, dishes, and even the kids. The soap also claims, among other things, to be used for curing any rash or hives, insect bites, and "dirty-mouthed kids." I think they were kidding about that last claim.

Three Civil War–era buildings that have been joined together to form Lehman's are stocked with more than 32,000 square feet of non-electric and historic tools, equipment, and furnishings.

From hundreds of cookie cutters to massive, wood-burning kitchen stoves; from a hand-powered water pump to glazed pottery mixing bowls, this non-electric mall also includes a bookstore as well as a food court where you can eat your lunch in an actual jail cell.

The cell came from the town jail in Somerset, Pennsylvania, which stood until the late 1800s and usually housed the town drunks and those caught gambling on Sundays. Jay Lehman picked it up many years ago as a curiosity, and it has now become a popular spot for families to sit in while eating their lunch.

From an Amish church bench to birdfeeders; from cast iron toy tractors to homemade candles; from a popcorn maker like Grandpa had to a hand-operated coffee grinder, if it doesn't need electricity, you might find it in Kidron.

Lehman's Hardware and Appliances
4779 Kidron Rd • Kidron, OH   888-438-5346
www.lehmans.com

For more things to see and do in the Kidron area, contact:

Wayne County Convention & Visitors Bureau
www.wccvb.com • 330-264-1800

Lighthouses of Lake Erie

Fairport Harbor, Lorain, Marblehead

I've always been fascinated by lighthouses. Perhaps it was because I spent my summers as a boy on the shores of Lake Erie. Lighthouses seem to capture our imagination. There are hundreds, perhaps thousands of poems, stories, books, and movies featuring iconic lighthouses, standing on a rocky shore, a vivid beacon in the darkest storm, a light to guide sailors to safety, a symbol of homecoming.

If you started counting lighthouses on Lake Erie, beginning with the historic structure on Marblehead Peninsula, and went totally around Lake Erie, you might be surprised to learn that there are 48 of these beacons in the night, nearly 20 in Ohio alone.

Of course, all lighthouses are not the same. Some are automated, sterile, modern versions of the sturdy structures that inspired hymns, songs, and poems; still others are replicas of long-ago lights that guided ships to a safe harbor. Some are retired and sit silent and dark, while others have been put to new work becoming icons and meccas of tourism.

The most prominent of these is the **Marblehead Lighthouse**, built way back in 1822. It is the oldest continuously operating lighthouse on the Great Lakes. Originally built of limestone to withstand the crashing waves of Lake Erie at the entrance to Sandusky Bay, it was 50 feet tall. Another 15 feet was added between 1897 and 1903, bringing its total height to 65 feet. The first lighthouse keeper was Revolutionary War veteran Benajah Wolcott. When he died in 1832, 10 years after the lighthouse began operating, his wife Rachel took over his duties, becoming the first female lighthouse keeper on the Great Lakes.

Today, the lighthouse is part of the Marblehead Lighthouse State Park, and in the spring, summer, and fall, tours are available. It is a great spot any time of year for a picnic and family photos.

You can see a modern replica of the 1877 Vermilion Lighthouse on the shore in front of the building that used to house the Inland Seas Maritime Museum at the Great Lakes Historical Society. While the replica lighthouse is not open for tours, it can easily be seen from the water and from the public beach at the end of Main Street.

Marblehead Lighthouse.

The new lighthouse, a smaller replica of the original, was put in place in 1992 by the museum.

However, if you want to see the original lighthouse, it still exists.

The 1877 lighthouse has a unique history, beginning with what it was made from. After the battle of Fort Sumter in the American Civil War, outdated cannons at the fort were melted down and used to construct the steel lighthouse destined for Vermilion.

In 1929, the lighthouse developed a list following a tough Ohio winter storm. The U.S. Army Corps of Engineers dismantled the lighthouse and, despite protests by local residents, left only a skeleton light on the pier. The rest of the lighthouse was hauled away.

Many years later, folks at the Great Lakes Museum discovered the lighthouse had been restored and put back to work, this time on Lake Ontario in New York, with a new name, the East Charity Shoal Light at Tibbet's Point, not far from Kingston, Ontario. It was finally retired in 2009 and, at last report, sold to a family from Texas who reportedly said they were going to make a summer home in the lighthouse. However, it is still used as an official beacon.

The **Lorain Lighthouse** is still one of the more picturesque guardians of the lake. Standing at the end of a long break wall, it can be accessed only by boat.

Built by the U.S. Army Corps of Engineers during the first World

War, in 1917, it functioned well into the 1960s before being replaced by a small-automated lighthouse on the tip of a newly constructed breakwall.

A civic group saved the building from demolition, and is working to restore the lighthouse They installed a wonderful lighting system that illuminates the structure in the evening, making it visible from most areas along the Lorain shoreline.

Today the lighthouse is owned by the Lorain Port Authority, which is working with the committee to restore the old building. Port Authority boats offer tours of both the exterior and sometimes the interior of the lighthouse during the warm months.

It was an earlier version of the lighthouse at the mouth of the Cuyahoga River in Cleveland harbor that is said to have inspired composer Philip Bliss in the late 1800s to write the hymn, "Let the Lower Lights Be Burning." The present-day lighthouse, built in 1910, is still used as an active lighthouse, and is inaccessible to the public.

But in Fairport Harbor, you can visit the first Great Lakes Lighthouse Marine Museum in the United States.

The **Fairport Harbor Lighthous**e, built in 1825, originally stood 30 feet high. Its size was doubled in 1871 when the tower was rebuilt with a spiral staircase with 69 steps that leads to an observation platform just below the light. The lighthouse was taken out of commission in 1925, when a new combination light and foghorn station was built on the west break wall of the harbor.

Besides the lighthouse, the lightkeeper's house serves as a museum and contains many exhibits pertaining to life on the Great Lakes. Attached to the museum is the pilothouse from a former Great Lakes carrier, the *Frontenac*.

Marblehead Lighthouse State Park
110 Lighthouse Dr • Marblehead, OH   419-734-4424
www.dnr.state.oh.us/parks/marblehead.htm

Lorain Lighthouse Tours
Lorain Port Authority, 319 Black River Lane • Lorain, OH   440-204-2269
www.lorainlighthouse.com

Fairport Harbor Marine Museum and Lighthouse
129 Second St • Fairport Harbor, OH   440-354-4825
www.fairportharborlighthouse.org

Shawshank and Ghosts

Mansfield

The first time I was ever in the Ohio State Reformatory in Mansfield, it was still an operating prison. No, I was not there as an inmate. I was visiting to do a story on a program they were offering to help rehabilitate prisoners. They offered a tour of the cell blocks while the men were at work, away from their cells. I remember well walking into the tiny steel cell. Once I was inside, the guard guiding me on the tour slammed the door shut and locked it. Although I knew I could get out, I felt a bubble of panic in my stomach.

The old, castle-like reformatory is now closed, and the prisoners moved to a modern prison about a mile away.

If you have ever seen the movie *The Shawshank Redemption*, you have seen the **Ohio State Reformatory** at Mansfield. The closed prison was used by Hollywood as the main set in the movie.

Today, the old prison is owned by a historical preservation society that gives tours, ghost walks, and even rents some of the rooms in the prison for weddings and reunions.

Three architectural styles, Gothic, Romanesque, and Queen Anne, were used by the architect in the design of the state prison when it was opened in 1896. More than 155,000 men served time here from the day it opened until the prison was closed in 1990, just a few years shy of its 100th birthday.

Although the architecture is creepy enough, when the giant wall with the guard sheds on top was still standing, it filled incoming inmates with despair. When the prison first closed, the state planned to demolish it.

The surrounding wall had been removed before the historical society was successful in taking over the structure and preserving the remaining historic buildings.

Now movie buffs and tourists from all over the world come here to walk through the huge cell blocks, see the solitary confinement cells, and gawk at the offices and rooms made familiar in the movie.

There is another building in downtown Mansfield that is also rich with history.

The Ohio State Reformatory at Mansfield. *(Rain0975, CC BY 2.0, goo.gl/enmKij)*

The Soldiers and Sailors Memorial Building opened at 34 Park Avenue West in 1889. It was built for veterans of the American Civil War, and even in recent years, offered meeting rooms to modern veterans' organizations on the ground floor.

Upstairs, the building has served other purposes. The town's first library was located here, and in 1889 the first museum in Richland County was started here.

The **Mansfield Memorial Museum** continues to this day.

On my last tour, museum director and curator Scott Schaut pointed out a part of a dead apple tree that purportedly was planted by John Chapman, the legendary "Johnny Appleseed."

The world's oldest surviving robot, "Elektro," built by Westinghouse Electric for the 1939 New York World's Fair, also is here.

There is a stunning display of over 600 model airplanes that once was displayed in the headquarters of the Ohio Air Guard at Mansfield Lahm Airport.

The museum boasts an eclectic collection that spans history from Roman times to the present.

Oh, did I mention that the place is haunted?

When I repeated the "haunted" rumor to Scott Schaut, he just pointed to a picture on the wall and said, "You are talking about Mr. Wilkinson."

Edward Wilkinson was the museum's first curator in the 1890s and

The Ohio State Reformatory at Mansfield has been used as a location for several movies. *(Tom Hart, CC BY 2.0, goo.gl/3N2iln)*

early twentieth century. Although he died many years ago, Mr. Wilkinson's spirit is believed to haunt the museum.

For example, Schaut said he moved some heavy display cases that Wilkinson had originally placed in a line on the second floor. They were moved about one foot over during cleaning and he discovered the cases had sat so long in one position that there was an indentation in the floor. The next day, when Schaut opened the doors, the cases were back in their original spots. No one had been there during the night.

Mansfield is a perfect One Tank Trip during the Halloween season.

The Ohio State Reformatory
100 Reformatory Rd • Mansfield, OH   419-522-2644
www.mrps.org

Mansfield Memorial Museum
34 Park Ave W • Mansfield, OH   419-525-2491
www.themansfieldmuseum.com

For more to do in Mansfield, check out:

Mansfield / Richland County Convention and Visitors Bureau
www.mansfieldtourism.com • 419-525-1300

Hidden Treasure on the Lake Shore

Mentor

Mentor has many fun and interesting things to see and do.

Remember the scene from the movie *The African Queen*, when Humphrey Bogart and Katharine Hepburn guided a small boat through a weed-choked river marsh? Well, you might feel a sense of *deja vu* as you set off on a kayak or paddleboard excursion through the edge of the **Mentor Marsh State Nature Preserve** next to the **Mentor Lagoons Nature Preserve & Marina**.

The canal where you start is lined with reeds that seem to stretch to the sky, nearly blocking out the sunlight. You can see birds and hear their calls as they flit through the cattails. You also paddle through the Mentor Lagoons, where you can see deer and other wildlife, as well as admire yachts and other boats docked in the city-owned marina. You might think you were in some exotic paradise, rather than a few hundred feet from the shores of Lake Erie.

The Mentor Lagoons Nature Preserve & Marina is a relatively new attraction. In 1998, the city purchased the land, along with a marina that can dock as many as 500 boats, to keep the property from being commercially developed. The preserve covers a 270-acre site tucked in just north of the larger, better-known Mentor Marsh State Nature Preserve. Located on a bluff overlooking Lake Erie, it contains 1½ miles of shoreline that includes both beach and dune plants.

The natural beach looks much as it did hundreds of years ago when Native Americans first discovered this area. On a warm summer day, it is a great place to relax and take one-of-a-kind photographs of the Lake County shoreline.

Above on the oak-studded bluff, more than three miles of hiking trails crisscross the forest and the wetlands below that feed into the giant, 600-acre-plus Mentor Marsh State Nature Preserve. Visitors can rent kayaks and paddleboards to explore the nearby waterways that make up the marina and parts of the marsh.

If you are a bird-watcher, you'll be interested to know that more than 150 species of birds have been sighted and recorded in the nature preserve.

Mentor Marsh State Nature Preserve. *(Erik Drost, CC BY 2.0, goo.gl/KHPTtz)*

It's also where many birds and butterflies nest each year, making it one of the top bird-watching sites in northern Ohio.

Mentor Marsh is the largest natural marsh left along the edge of Lake Erie, and became the state's first nature preserve in 1971.

Its trails and boardwalks let you wander, and it's a great place to see lots of wildlife and the migration of many kinds of birds.

Mentor Marsh State Nature Preserve Visitor Center
5185 Corduroy Rd • Mentor, OH   440-257-0777
www.cmnh.org

Mentor Lagoons Nature Preserve & Marina
8365 Harbor Dr • Mentor, OH   440-205-3625
www.cityofmentor.com

For other nearby attractions, see other chapters of this book or:

Lake County Visitors Bureau
www.lakevisit.com • 440-975-1234

Soaring Over Geauga County

Middlefield

I think every person who has ever spent a lazy summer afternoon watching a hawk spiraling through the sky must have felt some envy for this majestic bird, with its wings outstretched against majestic clouds, flying silently over earth spread out like a giant carpet below.

Well, you can actually experience this same feeling over northeastern Ohio—in a sailplane.

What is a sailplane?

Basically, it's an airplane without a motor that's towed on a long rope by an airplane with a motor to an altitude of 3,000 feet or better, then the rope is released. The sailplane can then be flown gently, silently, and safely back to earth.

But at the hands of an experienced pilot, the craft can stay up for long periods of time and even gain altitude by searching for updrafts, invisible columns of heated air, that rush upward from the earth. When found, they can give pilot and passenger the feeling that they have just stepped onto an elevator.

Gliding around the sky on these elusive columns of air, sailplane flights can sometimes last longer than an hour before gravity takes over and you have to return to the landing field.

The **Cleveland Soaring Society** has been around for more than 50 years and is based at the Geauga County Airport in Middlefield. On most weekends from April to October, weather permitting, you can find club members at the field flying their gliders.

Visitors are welcome and, for a nominal fee, members will even take you up for a ride in a two-passenger sailplane.

The flight starts near the end of the runway. A powered airplane is ahead of you. Once you are strapped in and the instructor/pilot climbs into the seat behind you, a ground crew member hooks the tow rope from the plane in front onto the glider, then lifts the wing of your craft and gives the signal to the pilot of the powered plane.

It's a bit bumpy as you start down the runway on the single wheel of the glider, then it becomes very smooth as you lift off the ground with the only sound the motor of the tow plane laboring ahead of you.

Instructor-Pilot Dave Tiber and I soar high over Middlefield in a sailplane.

As the planes steadily climb, buildings and trees appear smaller. When you reach 3,000 feet, the pilot tells you to pull a knob on the dashboard. There is a snap as the rope drops away, your aircraft, now freed, jerks upward slightly, and there is only the sound of the wind passing your canopy.

You fly in silence over homes and farms far below, conversing with the pilot in normal tones as you circle and crisscross the air space above the countryside.

All too soon, the ground starts getting closer. The pilot maneuvers the craft into a landing pattern and makes his final approach to the runway. It is a ride you won't soon forget.

Even if you are an experienced pilot, motorless flight is an adventure to be savored. It's a great way to spend a beautiful summer day.

Cleveland Soaring Society, Inc.
Geauga County Airport
15421 Old State Rd • Middlefield, OH   440-941-4277
www.clevelandsoaring.org

Middlefield is home to one of the largest Amish settlements in Ohio. For more ideas in the area, see other chapters in this book or:

Destination Geauga
www.destinationgeauga.com • 440-632-1538

Mohican Adventure

Loudonville

A very scenic part of Ohio is where Ashland and Holmes counties come together. It is called "Mohican Country."

Mohican Country was named for the Mohican Indians who once lived here. The name comes from the word "muheconneok," which means "from the waters that are never still." But Native Americans weren't talking about the Mohican River; they were referring to the Hudson River in New York.

You see, when James Fenimore Cooper wrote his novel *The Last of the Mohicans*, he created a lot of confusion by getting two tribes—the Mahicans and the Mohegans—mixed up. He gave several Mahican characters Mohegan names, and now the name "Mohicans" is often applied to either tribe. The Mohicans are part of the Delaware tribe, which no longer has a presence in Ohio. But they are remembered in a state park that bears their name.

Mohican State Park comprises 1,110 acres of forests and fields with five miles of the scenic Clear Fork branch of the Mohican River running through it.

The park offers camping, hiking trails, river adventures, and even a 96-room lodge and resort with a restaurant and a swimming pool.

One thing the entire Mohican area is known for is canoes.

Back in the late 1950's Dick Frye, an avid outdoorsman, went on a canoe trip on a scenic river in Michigan. He loved it so much, he decided that he wanted to bring the sport to northern Ohio.

In 1961, with six canoes and a station wagon, Frye opened The **Mohican Canoe Livery** on the banks of the Black Fork River on Route 3, south of Loudonville and started a business that eventually brought a new identity, "The Canoe Capital of Ohio," to the sleepy little town that previously was better known as the place where buses were built.

Today, there are seven canoe liveries up and down the Black Fork and Mohican Rivers and on a nice summer day, thousands of canoes pack the placid streams, resembling I-71 at rush hour. But it is not just canoes anymore. Today, the canoes are joined by rafts, inner tubes, and kayaks.

One of the many canoe liveries in Mohican Country.

The Black Fork and the Mohican Rivers are rated Class 1 waterways, meaning they are usually shallow and slow moving, which makes them perfect for hand-powered watercraft. Rides downstream, when you don't really have to do much rowing, just steer the boat, can run as short as seven miles. A downstream ride can take up to two hours, or you can take a trip lasting several days.

As for Mohican Canoe Livery, where it all started, today it is known as Mohican Adventures and is still going strong, renting canoes and other watercraft to tourists who want a water adventure. In addition to canoes, kayaks, tubes, and rafts, they have added a miniature golf course and go-kart tracks. One of the latest features is an "aerial park" which has several climbing courses with different levels of challenges. Mohican Adventures also offers camping sites and even some luxury cabins with air conditioning and fireplaces, as well as a conference center.

Just outside of Loudonville, right next to the Mohican State Park, is Mohican State Forest, which covers more than 5,000 acres. One of its highlights is the scenic overlook from the park at Clear Fork Gorge, where an ancient glacier carved a channel through sandstone that created the Clear Fork of the Mohican River. The gorge is more than 1,000 feet wide at the top and 300 feet deep. The National Park Service has registered the site as a National Natural Landmark.

An overlooked attraction is the Memorial Forest Shrine honoring

Ohio's men and women who died in World War II, the Korean War, the Vietnam War, and the two Gulf Wars. It's a small, sandstone chapel that sits in the midst of 310,000 trees planted in memory of the 20,000 Ohioans who made the supreme sacrifice. Inside the shrine are two books containing the names of those who lost their lives in the conflicts. Admission is free; the shrine is open during daylight hours.

Mohican State Park
3116 State Rte 3 • Loudonville, OH   419-994-5125
parks.ohiodnr.gov/mohican

Mohican Adventures Canoe Livery & Fun Center
3045 State Rte 3 • Loudonville, OH   419-994-4097
www.mohicanadventures.com

Treetop Adventure

Oberlin

The first thing you hear as you stand beside a tiny waterway in the Vermilion Valley is the birds.

Then you hear another noise: faint screams of elation, followed by a sound like a swarm of angry bees that grows louder and louder.

Suddenly, a person dangling from a thin wire flashes overhead high up in the trees.

This is **Common Ground Canopy Tours** near Oberlin, which some say is one of the best zip line courses in the Buckeye State. The tour covers nearly 40 acres of woods and, weather permitting, is one of the few zip line courses open most of the year.

Anyone over the age of 10 and weighing between 70 and 250 pounds can do the canopy tour; however, you must sign a waiver and pass a ground school session in which you learn safety rules and demonstrate to the guides that you can operate the apparatus that carries you on the zip line.

The adventure begins as, wearing a special harness, you climb a series of stairs to the top of a four-story-platform. You clip onto a small trolley mounted on a single steel cable and are launched on the first of seven zip lines that carry you through and above some trees to each of 13 tree platforms high above the forest ground. In the 2½ to 3 hours that you are in the trees, you will cross three narrow aerial bridges and climb staircases spiraled around the trunks of two large trees, taking you ever-higher into the treetops. If your adrenalin is not pumping hard enough, you'll also climb a rare floating staircase. It's hard to describe this stairway, but it is usually the "OMG" moment in the entire adventure.

When you get to the next to the last tree stand, you take one of the longest zip lines through the forest and across a branch of the Vermilion River to the final tree stand, where one last challenge awaits you: you clip onto a rope and rappel to the ground below, a distance of about 25 feet.

This part of the Vermilion River Valley is beautiful in just about every season, but especially in autumn, when the trees are ablaze with

A zip line rider prepares to soar over the Vermilion River.

red, orange, and brown. Both wild turkey and deer have been spotted by people sailing through the forest, high above the river and ground.

Common Ground calls itself "an experiential learning center," and offers other programs to help guests push their perceived limits: rope courses and a fire walk, where guests are invited to walk through red hot coals in their bare feet.

Common Ground Canopy Tours
14240 Baird Rd • Oberlin, OH   440-707-2044
www.commongroundcenter.org

For other ideas in the area check out:

Lorain County Visitors Bureau
www.visitloraincounty.com • 440-984-5282

The Little Park That Could

New Philadelphia

Tuscora Park is one of those hidden gems that makes a small town unforgettable. You might say that Tuscora Park is a work in progress. It began in the early 1900s, when J. E. Reeves, a prominent local man, decided the community of New Philadelphia needed a park and a place to swim. A few years later, the park was sold to the city. The entryway was redeveloped by the Work Projects Administration during the Great Depression. This site once housed a dance hall and a zoo; now it offers a compact amusement park that has created childhood memories for generations of kids in Tuscarawas County.

My first One Tank Trip to Tuscora Park was in the early 1990s. I was immediately struck by the beauty of the place. Its amphitheater takes advantage of the rolling hills of this part of Ohio, and there are a small lake and an Olympic-sized swimming pool. The air is filed with screams of fun coming from the amusement park rides.

There is a kiddie roller coaster that also allows adults to ride and a small train that takes passengers, big and little, past the lake where ducks and seagulls gather. You'll also find a handful of kiddie rides where youngsters can steer cars and miniature airplanes.

Overlooking the amusement park is a Ferris wheel that some claim the city inherited after a train carrying it to another destination had an accident in town. For some reason, the Ferris wheel was left behind when the damage was cleaned up, and the train went on its way.

And then there is the park's venerable carousel. Purchased in 1941, it is a rare all-wooden- animal merry-go-round, built in the 1920s in Tonawanda, New York.

Legend has it that this is the longest carousel ride in Ohio, or perhaps the whole country. As one happy youngster told me, "You ride so long, you're bound to hurl." I asked Carey Gardner of the local Rotary Club, which operates the concession rides for the city, about the boy's statement. He just grinned and said, "That may have been true in the past, but when we renovated the motor on the carousel a couple of years ago, besides making it a smoother ride, we also installed a timer that usually cuts the ride off at five minutes now."

Speaking of the Rotary Club, they stepped in several years ago when it appeared that the city could no longer afford to keep the amusement rides because of spiraling costs of insurance and repairs. By forming a private non-profit corporation, the service club was able to take over the operation and keep the rides going. All profits are poured right back into maintenance and even new rides.

Besides the rides, there are concession stands. Scott Robinson, president and CEO of the Tuscarawas County Chamber of Commerce, pointed out that hundreds of local kids have found their first job at Tuscora Park, either running the rides or selling hot dogs, hamburgers, and cotton candy to the visitors.

The best news is there is no admission charge to the park. You only pay for using the rides or some of the concessions, such as the batting cages that were added in recent years. The Rotary Club has also kept the prices affordable for families.

Tuscora Park is open year-round, but the amusement rides are only open from Memorial Day to Labor Day.

Tuscora Park
161 Tuscora Ave NW • New Philadelphia, OH   330-343-4644
www.newphilaoh.com

For more ideas in the area, see other chapters in this book or:

Tuscarawas County Convention & Visitors Bureau
www.traveltusc.com • 800-527-3387

The merry-go-round at Tuscora Park offers a long ride. *(Andy Donaldson Photography)*

Ohio's Little Switzerland

Dover, Sugarcreek

Many Swiss immigrants made their way to the rolling hills and valleys of Tuscarawas County in the 1830s. The reason: it reminded them of Switzerland. So many Swiss settled in the little town of Sugarcreek that today it is known as "Ohio's Little Switzerland."

The centerpiece of this town is the **World's Largest Cuckoo Clock**, which sits in a small park at Main Street and Broadway.

The clock originally was part of a restaurant complex in nearby Wilmot known as Alpine-Alpa. It was built in the early 1970s.

When the restaurant closed in 2009, the clock was put up for auction. A Walnut Creek businessman bought the huge timepiece and eventually gave it to the village of Sugarcreek.

The long-time tourist favorite was featured on the cover of the 1977 *Guinness Book of World Records.*

It is 23 feet tall and 24 feet wide, and many parts were imported from Switzerland. A hand-carved wooden band marches out of openings in the clock face every half-hour when the cuckoo comes out. As the band plays, two carved dancers do a Swiss dance.

When the clock was at the restaurant, it was located on a hillside behind the building. It cost 25 cents to see the hourly ceremony with the carved figures. Today, it is free. The clock runs year-round, but the dancing figures are shut down in extremely cold weather.

A majority of the shops and stores downtown are built in the style of traditional Swiss architecture. Even the pay telephone booth on the square resembles a miniature chalet. Beautiful three-dimensional murals of Switzerland adorn many businesses, restaurants, and banks.

The murals are the work of a local self-taught artist, Tom Miller, who spent much of his life painting scenes of Switzerland and the Sugarcreek area on the fronts, sides and ceilings of businesses in Tuscarawas and Holmes Counties. Miller is also responsible for the Swiss look of the downtown. In 1953, following the first Swiss Festival held in the community, Miller remodeled a downtown building he owned and gave it a Swiss façade. Over the years, other merchants followed

World's Largest Cuckoo Clock, now at home in Sugarcreek.

suit. Miller passed away in 1996, but his memory and his art lives on in his murals.

The Swiss brought with them their abilities to make Emmentaler, or as we call it, "Swiss" cheese, the delicious, nutty-flavored variety with the holes in it. Incidentally, those holes are caused during fermentation, which creates pockets of gas within the cheese while it is curing. When the process dissipates, it leaves the trademark holes.

For more than 80 years, the **Broad Run Cheesehouse and Swiss Heritage Winery** has been one of the places producing the cheese that helped make Sugarcreek famous. Over the years, Broad Run has won blue ribbons for its cheese in a competition for the title of "Ohio's Grand Champion Swiss Cheese." They offer tours of their factory on weekday mornings.

A few years ago, they opened the Swiss Heritage Winery on the factory grounds. The winery offers more than a dozen varieties of wines with innovative names: "Hans's Favorite," and "Back to the 40s Red Wine." They also make cranberry and blueberry wines. In the wine-tasting room in the Cheesehouse retail store, you can sample their wines and cheeses.

Folks in Sugarcreek celebrate their heritage each year with the annual Swiss Festival featuring family activities such as yodeling contests, a giant parade, the blowing of the huge alpenhorns, and a steinstassen contest. "Steinstassen" is Swiss for rock throwing.

Contestants take turns heaving a nearly 60-pound boulder to see who can throw it farthest. (Hey! Those guys herding the cattle up in the Alps had to do something to pass the time.) The festival is one of the best in Ohio, and attracts thousands to the small town each autumn.

Sugarcreek is also the eastern gateway to Ohio's Amish Country. It's not unusual to see the horses and buggies of the Amish traveling over village streets. In fact, Sugarcreek is home to *The Budget*, the Amish-oriented newspaper that is mailed weekly to Amish families around the world.

Amish influence is also seen in businesses such as **Beachy's Country Chalet Restaurant** on the eastern edge of Sugarcreek. Amish- and Swiss-style cooking draws tourists daily for home-style turkey and beef dinners, along with fresh-from-the-oven pies, and other made-from-scratch goodies such as date pudding and homemade soups.

You will find Swiss and the Amish cultures blending together in this community: in a museum that traces the history of Ohio cheese-making, small shops that sell all kinds of handmade crafts and furniture, and stores that sell bulk foods and homemade fudge.

World's Largest Cuckoo Clock
100 N Broadway St • Sugarcreek, OH   330-852-4112
www.villageofsugarcreek.com

Broad Run Cheesehouse and Swiss Heritage Winery
6011 Old Rte 39 NW • Dover, OH   800-332-3358
www.broadruncheese.com

Beachy's Country Chalet Restaurant
115 Andreas Dr NE • Sugarcreek, OH   330-852-4840

Cod in Lake Erie

Cleveland

There is a cod in Lake Erie, but it is not a fish.

The **USS *Cod*** (SS-224), a World War II fleet submarine, has been part of the Cleveland shoreline since the 1950s. It was deployed on seven wartime patrols and credited with sinking 12 enemy vessels and the rescue of a Dutch submarine crew who became stranded on a reef in the South China Sea. The submarine was brought to Cleveland through the St. Lawrence Seaway to be used as a training vessel for the U.S. Naval Reserve personnel.

When the navy deemed the ship no longer useful in the 1970s, it was earmarked for demolition when a group of Clevelanders formed the Cleveland Coordinating Committee to Save *Cod*.

I am proud to have been an early supporter of the group and to have assisted them in getting publicity for their effort to keep the ship from being torn up for scrap. They succeeded, and in the mid-1970s the navy gave guardianship of the submarine to the group. It opened as a floating memorial in May 1976.

Today, the submarine is much as it was during its fighting days. In fact, it is the only World War II submersible that hasn't had doors or stairways cut into the body of the ship. Visitors use the same narrow ladders that sailors used 70 years ago to get from the deck to the various rooms and departments within the ship.

In 1986, the USS *Cod* was designated a National Historical Landmark by the U.S. Department of the Interior, and is considered one the finest examples of World War II submarines on public display. While it serves as a memorial for the 3,900 submariners who lost their lives in the more than 100 years of the submarine service, the *Cod* is also a major tourist attraction in downtown Cleveland.

The ship is 312 feet long and weighs 1,525 tons, and was built in 1942 in Groton, Connecticut. It carried a crew of seven officers and 69 enlisted men when it was commissioned.

Today, you can see the cramped quarters that the men shared and look through a periscope. Unlike movie versions of the large room where the periscope was raised and lowered, in real life, the periscope

The USS *Cod* has been kept in her original World War II condition.

is located in a cramped and tiny space above the main area of the submarine.

One surprising item in the galley (the kitchen) of the ship is an ice cream machine. Apparently, these young sailors would give up many luxuries to be part of a submarine crew, but ice cream was not one of them.

Many of the volunteers and guides on the *Cod* today are submarine veterans and have first-hand stories to share with visitors.

USS Cod
1089 E 9th St • Cleveland, OH   216-566-8770
www.usscod.org

Vermilion's Best Kept Secret

Vermilion

Each day in summer, thousands of people drive by and hardly notice the gates to **Linwood Park**. Located next to the upscale Vermilion Lagoons, where the wealthy steer their yachts up to their front doors, this small, private resort sits on a tree-shaded bluff overlooking both the lagoons and Lake Erie.

Linwood Park was founded in the late 1800s by an evangelical group that wanted to duplicate, in a smaller way, Chautauqua Lake in New York and Lakeside on the Marblehead Peninsula in Ohio.

With what some have called the finest privately owned beach on Lake Erie, Linwood Park consists of 60 acres of mostly two-story homes called "cottages." Many were built in the 1800s, and all are privately owned, many by the same family for generations. Some are available for rent from the individual owners.

It's a tranquil, family place of shaded streets and tradition, a sort of portal to the past. (I spent the summers of my youth at Linwood Park. It was an idyllic place to grow up in.)

Besides the beach, which was the original attraction, the Park also has a large tabernacle and chapel where religious services, weddings, meetings, and other events are held. There are shuffleboard, basketball, and volleyball courts, and a large children's playground with a mock-up of a pirate ship, slides, and swings.

"The Stand" is a Park icon. It's an ice cream parlor, souvenir stand, and convenience store rolled into one. Sleeping rooms upstairs are the only accommodations in the Park you can rent for a night or a week. Next door, a building that was once the Linwood Park grocery store now serves as part museum and part craft store, selling items hand-made by Park residents.

Linwood Park residents and visitors alike pay an entry fee during the summer months; however, if you just want to look around and perhaps get an ice cream cone at the Stand, you can leave your driver's license at the gate and spend up to an hour and a half in the park at no cost. After that time, you'll pay the daily fee.

Just outside the gates and across the Vermilion River, you will find

Parson's Marina, home of the ***Mystic Belle***. The tiny mock-paddle wheel boat carries about 21 people on hour-long tours of the river, Vermilion lagoons, and the mouth of the harbor, which empties into Lake Erie. Captain Don Parsons is a long-time Vermilion resident who has many stories to tell about the river and the town.

You can't visit Vermilion without trying another tradition, **Brummer's Homemade Chocolates**. The company was founded in New Jersey in 1904; Bob and Sandy Brummer opened their Vermilion store more than 25 years ago, and it has been the go-to place for homemade chocolates ever since. Bob and Sandy even put me to work during one Christmas season, pulling molten candy on a hook to make a batch of candy canes. I found out very quickly that old-fashioned candy making, the way the Brummer's do it, is really hard work. You can't beat the taste. After almost every trip to Vermilion, I go home with a box of Brummer's Homemade Chocolates.

Linwood Park
4920 Liberty Ave • Vermilion, OH   440-967-4237
www.linwoodpark.org

Mystic Belle Cruises
636 Sandusky St • Vermilion, OH   440-967-7910
www.donparsonsmarina.com

Brummer's Homemade Chocolates
672 Main St • Vermilion, OH   440-967-2329
www.brummers.com

Linwood Park, an idyllic place in the summer.

Zebras, Camels, and Other Exotic Friends

Vienna

It was a beautiful day, with puffy clouds floating through a blue sky. The huge camouflaged open vehicle meandered down a gravel road, winding its way through fields and past lakes where antelope were knee-deep in the water, drinking. The truck was followed by camels, Watusi cattle, zebras, and a host of other exotic creatures. The youngsters on board squealed with delight as the truck lumbered down the bank of a waterway, waded through the hubcap-deep water, and finally pulled up onto a small rise where llamas and mountain goats were waiting.

The Serengeti? No. Vienna, Ohio.

This is **Wagon Trails Animal Park**, not far from Youngstown, and it gives visitors the chance to feel they might be in Africa or on several other continents as animals from around the world crowd the specially designed trucks.

Each visitor is given a bucket filled with food pellets that the animals crave, so it's not unusual to see tiny pot-bellied pigs running between the clumsy hooves of camels, or zebras shoulder to shoulder with a water buffalo, all hoping passengers will toss them a treat.

Wagon Trails Animal Park was once a dairy farm, where herds of black and white Holstein cattle grazed. Now the 70 acres of pasture and woods are home to nearly 500 exotic animals from six continents.

Alex Bertok, the owner of this virtual Noah's Ark, says his son suggested that it might be more profitable to give up their home supply business and farming enterprise to start an animal park where visitors could get up close and personal with creatures that they usually have seen only in books or from a distance at a zoo.

So in 1999, Wagon Trails Animal Park was born. At first the preserve had only about 150 animals, ranging from antelope to cattle and bison. The original way for visitors to tour the park was on a horse-drawn wagon, but Alex says they stopped that because the horses were sometimes frightened by the wild turkeys in the enclosure and there were spiraling insurance rates to use the horse-drawn wagons.

Wherever the Safari Wagon stops, the animals gather.

They decided to replace the horses and wagons and build their own safari vehicles from surplus military trucks.

The vehicles range in size from the familiar "deuce-and-a-half" trucks that can carry between 35 and 40 people at a time, all the way up to a giant semi-tractor-trailer with a capacity of 150 to 200 passengers. "Boy Scouts and Girl Scouts love the big truck because their entire group can ride together," says Alex Bertok. The specially designed vehicles are open, but with sides that protect the visitors if any animal tries to climb on board.

One highlight of the tour is a stop on a bridge between two ponds filled with giant koi. When a bucket of food is dumped onto the surface of the pond, the water roils with fish scrambling for their share of the chum.

Another favorite moment is when the big vehicles pull up to the edge of a large pond, then drive off the edge into the water, splashing across an underwater ford to an island where more animals are awaiting a treat.

"The water crossing has been so popular that we are thinking of adding a tunnel under a hill out here where we would drive underneath the animals," Bertok says.

The final stop on the nearly hour-long tour is Ostrich Alley, where the inquisitive, long-necked, seven-foot-tall birds try to dive into the outstretched buckets of food held by visitors.

In addition to the tour there is also a petting zoo of baby animals, where you will find peacocks, baby ostrich, kangaroo, miniature horses, and a host of regular farm animal young.

Wagon Trails Animal Park is open from May through the end of October. There is an admission fee and, by the way, take cash: They do not accept credit or debit cards or personal checks. An ATM machine is available on the premises.

It was just after lunch when we left the animal park and, at the suggestion of Alex Bartok, we stopped to eat at the **Yankee Kitchen Restaurant**, about a half-mile from the park.

This small country diner features quick service, moderate prices, and food that is a cut above what you'll find in the usual small town eatery. The salads were enormous, and could have served two or more. Yankee Kitchen has also won some area contests for its hamburgers.

Wagon Trails Animal Park
907 Youngstown-Kingsville Rd SE • Vienna, OH   330-539-4494
www.wagontrails.com

The Yankee Kitchen Restaurant
484 Youngstown-Kingsville Rd • Vienna, OH   330-394-1116
www.facebook.com/theyankeekitchen

Center of the World and Other Unusual Stops

Warren

The center of the world is in Ohio. Just ask about anyone in Trumbull County in the northeastern section of the state.

As you approach the intersection of State Routes 5 and 82, a familiar green-and-white state department of highways sign proclaims that you are, indeed, in the **Center of the World**.

Actually, you are in a small, unincorporated community in Braceville Township in Trumbull County. The community of Center of the World was founded in Ohio's pioneer days by an eccentric investor named Randall Wilmot who hoped to make this frontier community a major trading center as the state started to develop and grow. Sadly for Mr. Wilmot, the railroads chose to pass through nearby Warren and that left Center of the World in the proverbial dust.

Today, there is not much to see in the community, but the road sign has become a regular stop for tourists who like to have their photo taken at the Center of the World.

Speaking of Warren, there is a really unusual tribute to a local son who became a rock-and-roll legend, David Grohl: rock musician, producer, and songwriter, who is best known as the front man of the rock group Foo Fighters.

Born in Warren, Grohl started out as a drummer, and was honored by his hometown with a set of **giant drumsticks** that were so big, they made the *Guinness World Records*.

The hand-carved drumsticks, as big as two telephone poles and weighing about 900 pounds, have been displayed in many parts of the town, but found a permanent home when the city also decided to name not a street, but an alley in Grohl's honor.

It is a bit hard to find, but near the intersection of the two main streets, Mahoning and West Market, you can find Grohl Alley. The drumsticks are about halfway down the alley and beneath two huge air-conditioning units mounted in a brick building.

There is a more complex memorial to a man who once lived in Warren as a boy. You can see a half-size scale replica of the Lunar

Excursion Module (LEM) that Neil Armstrong used when he became the first man to step on the surface of the moon.

The **First Flight Lunar Module** is located on U.S. Route 422, right next to a McDonald's Restaurant. This site was the Warren airport when six-year-old Neil Armstrong lived in Warren, where Stephen Armstrong took his son for his very first airplane ride in a Ford Tri-Motor airplane. The replica, believed to be the only one of its kind, was built in 2001. In 2005, Neil Armstrong visited the site and gave it a thumbs-up for its detail and workmanship.

Center of the World Road Sign
Intersection of Ohio Rte 82 and 5 • Braceville Township, OH

David Grohl's Giant Drumsticks
Grohl's Alley • Warren, OH

First Flight Lunar Module
2553 Parkman Rd NW • Warren, OH   330-898-3456
www.firstflightwarren.org

For other interesting things to see and do in the Warren/Trumbull County area, contact:

Trumbull County Tourism Bureau
www.exploretrumbullcounty.com • 330-675-3081

A selfie at the Center of the World.

NORTHWEST OHIO

Cars and Trucks of the Past

Bowling Green, Woodville

If you have ever dreamed of again owning the first car you ever drove or if you just like classic automobiles or racing cars, this One Tank Trip is for you.

The destination: one of Ohio's finest privately-owned auto museums.

Snook's Dream Cars is housed in a museum with the entryway disguised as a head-turning replica of a 1940s-era Texaco Service Station, complete with glass-top gasoline pumps. The display of 30-plus classic automobiles is the private collection of Bill and Jeff Snook, a father-and-son team that started restoring cars back in 1963, when Bill Snook helped his son Jeff to restore a 1929 Model "A" Ford. It became Jeff's transportation when he turned 16.

As he grew older, Jeff started racing automobiles. Several of his classic race cars are on display along with cars dating from the 1930s through the 1960s. But that's just part of the collection. Jeff Snook told me they have more cars in storage and try to rotate them onto the museum floor every few weeks. Another feature that impressed me was that every car on display sparkles as though it had just been driven off the assembly line.

Along with the cars is a huge collection of auto memorabilia such as hood ornaments and door handles that fills display cases,

Just a few of the unusual cars in the eclectic collection at Snook's Dream Cars.

and the museum also features larger collectibles: pinball machines, jukeboxes, and animated kiddie rides that, like the cars, have been restored to working order. The interior of the old service station look-a-like is decorated with street scenes from Bowling Green of years ago and even had a Sebring Raceway Pit Lane.

But Snook's Dream Cars is not just a museum. The Snooks also operate a business here restoring classic cars in the four-bay mechanics' area. In addition, they have a new warehouse with more than 6,000 square feet of climate-controlled storage available for rent to other classic car collectors, and they also sell classic and collectible cars of all kinds.

Sadly, Bill Snook passed away in 2013 at the age of 91, but Jeff continues to operate the business and museum.

Bowling Green is also home to another rather unusual museum of motorized history whose motto is: "Working to preserve the history of the construction equipment that shaped our world." If you have someone in the family who has ever worked in the construction industry or a youngster who just loves trucks and caterpillars, this is the place for you.

The **Historical Construction Equipment Association** has a museum of antique heavy equipment located just outside of town at their headquarters on Liberty Hi Road. Here you will find everything from a horse-drawn grader used to smooth roads in the early years of the twentieth century to a working restored model of a giant Marion 21 Electric Shovel manufactured in 1926. In all, there are more than 50 exhibits, inside and out; many have been restored to like-new working condition by volunteers. If you would like to see some of these historic machines at work, each autumn, the annual Great Lakes Logging & Heavy Equipment Exposition is held on the museum grounds. You can see many different pieces of equipment, from graders to giant shovels, doing their thing.

The museum is open weekday afternoons. Call for an appointment.

While we are on the subject of classic cars, there is a drive-in restaurant that I recommend.

You can't miss the **Speedtrap Diner** in nearby Woodville.

There's a 1950s-era police car parked on the roof.

The diner got its name because over the years, the small town gained a reputation for being a speed trap for motorists who ignored the speed limit, which was strictly enforced by local police.

Owner Samantha Haar also is a big fan of the 1950s—so much so that she has life-size figures of Elvis Presley and Marilyn Monroe in the restrooms. But that is just the beginning. The walls and even the ceiling of the dining room are covered with memorabilia of the era.

Samantha is the head cook, and she aims to please. While the menu is heavy on burgers, there are daily specials, and Samantha frequently comes up with new ice cream flavors.

It's a fun place.

Snook's Dream Cars
13920 County Home Rd • Bowling Green, OH   419-353-8338
www.snooksdreamcars.com

Historical Construction Equipment Museum
16623 Liberty Hi Rd • Bowling Green, OH   419-352-5616
www.hcea.net

Speedtrap Diner
310 E. Main St • Woodville, OH   419-849-3665
www.speedtrapdiner.com

For more ideas in the area, contact:

Bowling Green Convention & Visitors Bureau
www.visitbgohio.org   419-372-2336

Rails of History

Bellevue

Bellevue has a long history with railroads, dating back to 1839, when the first railroad chartered in the state was the Mad River and Lake Erie Railroad that ran from Sandusky to Bellevue. It later became a major train yard on the Nickel Plate Railroad, and today has one of the best railroad museums in Ohio, if not the entire Midwest.

The **Mad River & Nickel Plate Railroad Museum** was established in 1976. It sprawls on both sides of Southwest Street, just alongside the operating rail tracks of the present-day Norfolk and Southern Railroad.

The museum grounds hold more than two dozen pieces of rolling stock, including diesel and steam-driven locomotives, boxcars of every description, refrigerated cars, mail cars, and even cars used to carry troops in time of war. There are luxurious passenger cars, some historic and some from later years, when major travel was still done by train.

Almost all the cars and locomotives are open and have steps leading inside. Adults and especially children are invited to climb aboard and try out the engineer's seat on a giant diesel or climb to the top of the observation area of a caboose and see the view once held by the train's conductor.

You can get a taste of yesterday as you walk into the wooden building that was once the Wheeling and Lake Erie Railroad's Curtice Depot. Here, you can see the small room where passengers waited for their train, the telegrapher's office, and even a pot-bellied stove that kept the place warm during a cold Ohio winter.

My favorite exhibits are in the museum, across the street.

As you enter, you are greeted by a replica of the very first locomotive that chugged into Bellevue nearly 200 years ago. The *Sandusky* was tiny, compared to today's giant diesel locomotives.

In a nearby glass case is a bell from a locomotive. It is believed that this bell was used on the Lincoln funeral train.

When President Abraham Lincoln was assassinated in 1865, his body was taken on a circuitous train trip from Washington to its final

The Mad River and NKP Railroad Museum has more than fifty pieces of railroading equipment on display.

resting place in Springfield, Illinois. More than 24 different locomotives pulled the cars carrying the president's body, so it is hard to prove that this bell actually came from one of them. However, museum officials say it was found in the possession of an ardent Lincolnia collector who felt certain his bell had the Lincoln connection. Rail historians say the bell is of the right era.

You'll also see uniforms, glassware, and other items used during the golden age of rail travel.

The museum and rail collection are open seasonally. If you have a railroad fan in the family, this is certainly the One Tank Trip for you.

Mad River & NKP Railroad Museum
253 Southwest St • Bellevue, OH   419-483-2222
www.madrivermuseum.org

For more suggestions for things to do in the area, see other chapters in this book or:

The Bellevue Area Tourism and Visitor's Bureau
www.bellevuetourism.org   419-684-4030

A Real Candy Land

Bryan

Bryan is called "The Fountain City" because it once had many artesian wells that bubbled out of the earth. In fact, today, the city water is provided by seven artesian wells, and residents brag about the taste of their city water.

Perhaps this pure water supply was one of the reasons the **Spangler Candy Company** came to Bryan. While you might not be familiar with Spangler, one of their products, Dum-Dum lollipops, is known the world over.

Now, lollipops are big business; the Spangler Bryan plant is huge. They make 2.3 billion Dum-Dums—that's billion with a "b"—each year. There are 16 flavors, and new ones are constantly being developed in their laboratory kitchen at the factory.

In case you are wondering, some of those that didn't make the cut were bacon and pepperoni.

Spangler encourages visitors to its company museum and store to sample and give their opinion about some of the new flavors. Its 500,000 square feet of buildings cover several city blocks, and with more than 425 employees, the company is one of the largest employers in the community.

They not only make lollipops, but also other standbys of the candy world such as Circus Peanuts, those little orange marshmallow creations that look like peanuts in the shell, and Saf-T-Pops, a lollipop with a handle in the shape of a loop for tiny hands. Spangler is also America's largest producer of candy canes.

It's the kind of place where workers seem to pass their jobs down from one generation to the next. From CEO Dean Spangler, who is the third generation to run this family-owned business, to E-Commerce Manager Mattea St. John, whose great-grandmother once worked on the candy line at the factory, just as Mattea did when she was in college.

Spangler Candy is also one of the few factories in Ohio that still gives tours. Two miniature Dum-Dum trolleys run every half-hour during the day, taking visitors to the factory on a ride through parts

On the factory tour at Spangler Candy Company, home of the Dum-Dum lollipop.

of the plant, packing room, and warehouse where tons of lollipops are stacked, waiting to be shipped all over the world.

While the trolleys won't take you into the actual candy-making areas, lots of video and photos in the company store show how the candy is made.

If you have a favorite flavor of Dum-Dums, you can find boxes of that single flavor at the museum store.

Spangler Candy Company
400 N Portland St • Bryan, OH   419-636-4221
www.spanglercandy.com

For more ideas in the area, see other chapters in this book or:

Bryan Chamber of Commerce
www.bryanchamber.org   419-636-2247

The Mystery of the Blue Hole

Castalia

From the 1920s to the 1990s, thousands of tourists' cars sported a bumper sticker or a window decal that proclaimed: "We've been to the mysterious Blue Hole."

The Blue Hole was a scenic pond in Castalia. People would go there to stare into its luminescent water. There wasn't anything in the water. No fish; just water. It was one of those tourist attractions that ranked up there with "Mystery Hill, where the water runs uphill" or "Home of the two-headed calf." The Blue Hole. It's one of those slightly off-center tourist attractions that sticks in your mind decades later.

I'm happy to report that new generations can still see a mysterious **Blue Hole** in Castalia. But first, a story about how it all started.

Ohio's Blue Hole was discovered by a non-Native American in 1761. Maj. Robert Rogers, leader of the famed "Rogers Rangers" of the French and Indian War, stumbled across it while on the way back from taking command of Fort Detroit. Native Americans had known for centuries about the strange water hole, believing it to have curative powers.

It's true that the water, which averaged 50 degrees year-round, never froze, came from deep in the earth, and contained no oxygen, so fish and other aquatic life couldn't survive in the pool.

All sorts of legends grew up around the pond. Some said it was bottomless; some claimed animals as big as cows had fallen into the pool, never to be seen again.

In reality, its depth was about 40 to 50 feet where the Blue Hole was fed from an underground stream.

The underground river runs toward Lake Erie with such force that it ate away the surrounding limestone and allowed a giant sinkhole to open in the earth.

The modern-day owner of the land where the Blue Hole was located, a trout club, pumped the water into its nearby fish hatchery, where it was aerated and used for raising fish for the anglers.

The trout club also made money by allowing the public to visit the Blue Hole. For a fee, they could admire the circular pond, stroll

This is the new Blue Hole discovered when the state took over the hatchery near the original Blue Hole.

the well-kept grounds, see the process of raising fish, and even feed popcorn to the young trout in the many manmade streams that criss-crossed the hatchery.

They could also stop at a small souvenir stand and, for a fee, take home that ubiquitous bumper sticker that proclaimed they had been to the Blue Hole.

Sadly, the attraction was forced to close its gates in the 1990s when compliance with new laws for public access to attractions became too costly. It appeared that the Blue Hole had slipped silently into tourist history.

But in 1997, the State of Ohio took over 90 acres next to the trout club where the original Blue Hole was to create a state fish hatchery.

At the rear of the property, they discovered another Blue Hole, not quite as large as the original, but equally deep, cold, and mysterious.

They also revealed a secret about the original Blue Hole that only the local residents and some researchers had known: There wasn't just one Blue Hole; there were several dotted around Castalia. Only the largest one had been commercialized and opened to the public.

While the original Blue Hole remains closed, the state has built an observation deck over part of the newly discovered water hole and placed plaques nearby explaining the pool's origin.

You can also take a self-guided tour of the state fish hatchery, where thousands of fish are raised to be released in Ohio's lakes and streams. The best part is that admission is free when the hatchery is open.

While the new Blue Hole might not have the rustic charm of the original attraction, it already has a legend: A pick-up truck got too close to the edge and fell in and a crane had to be called to remove it from the depths of the pool.

While you are in the neighborhood, there is another place you might want to stop that serves some legendary french fries: **Berardi's Family Kitchen**.

For more than 50 years, the Berardi family sold french fried potatoes at Cedar Point Amusement Park. Today, the family operates a chain of restaurants bearing their name in the Sandusky area, and you can still order the french fries that used to draw customers to their stand on the Cedar Point midway. The restaurants offer a good variety of homemade foods, and are quite popular.

Blue Hole
Castalia State Fish Hatchery ODNR
7018 Homegardner Rd • Castalia, OH   419-684-7499

Berardi's Family Kitchen
1019 W Perkins Ave • Sandusky, OH   419-626-4592
www.sanduskyberardis.com

The First Presidential Library

Fremont

Ohio has a long list of presidents who have been born here.

Sadly, with the exception of William McKinley, William Howard Taft, and Warren G. Harding, who were early twentieth century presidents, the others—William Henry Harrison, Benjamin Harrison, Ulysses S. Grant, James A. Garfield and Rutherford B. Hayes—served in the nineteenth century and most are largely forgotten.

However, the son of President Rutherford B. Hayes started a tradition that continues today with our twenty-first century presidents: the tradition of a presidential library.

After serving one term as president, Rutherford B. Hayes lived out his remaining years on his estate, Spiegel Grove, in Fremont. "Spiegel" is the German word for mirror. The estate was named for the large puddles of rainwater that gather beneath the grove of huge trees on the estate and reflect, or mirror, the grove.

Col. Webb Hayes, the second son of the president, was a soldier and world traveler. When his father died, Webb and his siblings took over the 25-acre estate with its 31-room brick mansion and honored their father by building a museum and library on the estate to house his personal papers and books as well as memorabilia from the Hayes presidency, his time as a general in the Civil War, and his term as governor of Ohio. Opened in 1916, it was the first presidential library and museum. Today, it is the **Rutherford B. Hayes Presidential Center**.

Spiegel Grove looks today much as it did when President Hayes lived here. The impressive gates at the entrances to the estate also have a presidential connection. They once guarded the entrances to the White House.

The winding road to the museum passes massive trees, some bearing plaques. Many were originally planted by famous visitors.

In a quiet spot not far from the mansion is the gravesite of President Hayes and his wife Lucy.

A fence surrounds an imposing granite stone that simply bears the names of Rutherford and Lucy Hayes. No mention that he was once a general, governor of Ohio and president of the United States.

Incidentally, just outside the fence on a hillside by the grave is a smaller stone inscribed: "Old Whitey, a hero of 19 battles." It marks the grave of President Hayes's favorite horse, which he rode while in the Civil War and brought home when he returned to Fremont.

President and Mrs. Hayes were also responsible for another White House tradition that continues today, the White House Easter egg roll.

It started when some youngsters used to roll eggs down a hill next to the Capitol. When some congressmen complained the youngsters were ruining the grass and chased them away, President Hayes heard about it and he and his wife invited the kids to come to the White House to roll their eggs on the lawn. It has been going on every Easter since. A few years ago, the tradition was also started at Spiegel Grove.

Today, you can tour not only the library and museum, but also the Hayes home that has been renovated, taking many of the rooms back to the way they appeared when the president and Mrs. Hayes lived there.

Rutherford B. Hayes Presidential Center
1337 Hayes Ave • Fremont, OH   419-332-2081
www.rbhayes.org

For more ideas in the area, see other chapters in this book or:

Sandusky County Convention & Visitors Bureau
www.sanduskycounty.org • 800-255-8070

Rutherford B. Hayes Presidential Center. *(Rutherford B. Hayes Presidential Center)*

A Presidential Resort

Lakeside

There is a place on Lake Erie that attracted at least two U.S. presidents to spend some of their summer enjoying the cool breezes and the scenery and waters of the lake.

Historic **Lakeside Chautauqua** was one of the original resorts that combined religion with education, culture, entertainment, and recreation. The Chautauqua idea spread across the country in the nineteenth century.

Located in Ottawa County on the shores of Lake Erie on the Marblehead Peninsula, Lakeside was founded in 1873 by members of the Methodist church, originally, as a place to hold old-fashioned revival camp meetings.

The cool lake breezes on hot summer days attracted people from all over the country and, as the years went by, cottages were built and then a hotel. Tabernacles and auditoriums followed, allowing cultural attractions to be added; a community orchestra, nationally known religious leaders and other speakers, and entertainers arrived. The lake offered recreation: fishing, boating, and swimming.

The religious-based resort has always banned alcohol and that fact appealed to presidents who visited here.

William McKinley is reported to have contacted the Hotel Lakeside manager to arrange for a reunion of his Civil War regiment. According to a book written by Lakeside historian Eleanor Durr, President McKinley told the manager, "Our boys need some place where intoxicants cannot be had. They seem to want to recognize friends over a cup of beer. I want to get them away from it."

Rutherford B. Hayes and his wife Lucy also were visitors at Lakeside reunions. During her time as First Lady, Mrs. Hayes was known as "Lemonade Lucy" because she did not allow any alcohol in the White House. A photo from the Hayes Presidential Center in Fremont shows President Hayes in front of the Hotel Lakeside with fellow veterans of the Civil War at a reunion.

Today, while still a Methodist-based institution, with quaint Victorian cottages lining its tree shaded streets, the popular facility is

The gates to historic Lakeside.

open to the general public. During the summer months, Lakeside is a gated community with admission fees to the resort and to some of the events. Throughout the summer, there will be lectures, concerts, craft and art shows, classic car meets, plays, musicals, nationally known entertainers, and the Lakeside Symphony Orchestra.

In addition, visitors can take classes in working with stained glass, sailing, and other topics. Supervised children's programs allow kids to have fun while their parents enjoy the tennis courts or the beach. It also gives them time to take in cultural activities at Lakeside or tour the nearby Lake Erie Islands.

Once inside the gates, automobile parking is very limited and a bicycle is a good idea for getting around the miles of streets and narrow lanes. If you like, there's a bike shop that rents and repairs bicycles and also has golf carts and electric scooters for rent.

There are many things to see and do. There are shuffleboard and tennis courts. Ottawa County's only remaining movie theater, Orchestra Hall, offers family movies in an air-conditioned setting.

Businesses range from a toy shop and a kite store to women's specialty clothing stores and places to get an ice cream cone or fudge.

The resort has a wonderful small museum with displays that illustrate the history of Lakeside as well as nearby Johnson Island, which was a prisoner-of-war camp for Confederate officers during the Civil War.

When it comes to mealtime there are sandwich and pizza shops, tea rooms, coffee shops, and, for more formal dining, the historic Hotel Lakeside dining room is open to visitors.

While no alcohol is served on the grounds of Lakeside, just outside and in nearby Marblehead and Catawba Island, you will find many restaurants and stores as well as some well-known Lake Erie area wineries that do.

You can spend the night at the Hotel Lakeside, with its nineteenth century charm and screened porch overlooking the lake, or the more modern Fountain Inn.

There are bed and breakfasts also available. A campground with electrical and sewer hookups is within the park, and large groups can arrange to rent a dormitory on the resort property to save on lodging costs.

But the activities each June, July and August are what really attract so many people to history-filled Lakeside: from ballet to drama; music, from pop to classical; a chance to interact with noted lecturers; days filled with cultural enrichment and fun on the shores of Lake Erie. As one person told me, "It's the place where even presidents come to play and pray."

Lakeside Chautauqua
236 Walnut Ave • Lakeside, OH   419-798-4461
www.lakesideohio.com

For more ideas in the area, contact:

Lake Erie Shores and Islands Welcome Center
www.shoresandislands.com • 419-625-2984

Parasailing Over Lake Erie

Put-in-Bay

Over the years, my job has let me do a lot of wonderful and crazy things. I have flown twice with the Blue Angels, the U.S. Navy's precision flying team; I have taken the wheel on board the Goodyear blimp; I have become a locomotive engineer, driving a 44-ton diesel locomotive through a freight yard; I have even driven a Korean War–vintage tank. Once I was even talked into roping and hog-tying a young steer at a rodeo.

I must confess that every time I did something that was unique or dangerous, I was both excited and scared.

I have never thought of myself as a brave person. I try those white-knuckle activities simply because, well, I would be embarrassed if I refused. Besides, other people have done it. How scary could it be?

I found out the day we decided it was time I went parasailing over Lake Erie.

We had arranged the ride with the good folks who operate the parasail concession on the boardwalk at Put-in-Bay on South Bass Island in Lake Erie.

There are two ways to go parasailing. The one most people have seen pops up on the Internet and those TV shows that display home videos of people's most embarrassing moments. You know: The one where the person is on the shore, attached to a long rope tied onto a speedboat, the boat takes off at high speed, and the poor person on the other end of the rope is dragged across the beach, usually face-down, his nose digging a furrow in the sand.

That is not how they do it at **Put-In-Bay Parasail**.

Here, you are on board the boat, well out into the lake. You strap on a harness attached to a large parasail. As the boat accelerates, the parasail inflates and you are gently lifted off the boat into the air.

As the speed of the boat increases, the winch connecting you to the parasail lets out more rope and you climb higher and higher into the sky.

When you look down, the boat looks like a small toy and it's very quiet as you float along above the boat's faraway wake.

Parasailing over Lake Erie near Put-in-Bay.

On a clear day, people claim you might even see the Canadian shoreline nearly 40 miles away. I didn't see that, but I did notice huge lake freighters on the horizon.

But I wasn't thinking about scenery right then; I had noticed in the quiet of my flight that I could hear the creaking of the nylon harness holding me aloft. I could swear I could hear the nylon threads snapping and convinced myself that I was only minutes from plunging hundreds of feet into the green waters of Lake Erie.

I finally decided that at least I could get a couple of photographs before I plummeted into the lake. My camera was hanging around my neck, and I let go of my death grip with my right hand (clinging even tighter with my left hand), raised the camera to my eye, and snapped a couple of pictures.

When I went to take a third photo, I realized the camera had run out of film. (This was in the days before digital cameras.) Determined, I left the camera hang from my neck as I frantically dug out an unexposed roll of film from my pocket, wrapped my left arm around the rope to my harness, and, with great difficulty, managed to get the camera open and change the roll of film.

I shot 36 more photos, proud of myself to the point that I almost forgot I was going to drop out of the sky at any moment.

Just then, the line to the boat started to tremble and, before I could yell or scream, I realized that they were winding me back down onto the speeding boat.

As I got closer and closer to the water, I realized that I was still 100 feet behind the boat and that if the present rate of descent continued, I was going to hit the water, not the boat.

That's just what happened. One second, I was skimming along the top of the waves, and the next, my feet hit the water and I suddenly became a human surfboard.

But before I could worry about my camera, wallet, and wristwatch getting wet, I was whipped back into the sky as the boat sped up.

I later learned that my camera crew had talked the boat captain into giving me the unexpected dip in the water. Photographers sometimes have a weird sense of humor.

As I finally landed on the boat and was unharnessed, the captain asked me how I had enjoyed my flight.

I proudly told him how I had managed to change the film in my camera and continued to take photos while thinking I was going to crash into the lake.

He responded: "Last week I had an 85-year-old grandmother who took up two cameras and 12 rolls of film and didn't want to come down until she had shot all 12 rolls."

Put-in-Bay Parasail
341 Bayview Ave • Put-in-Bay, OH   419-285-3703
www.putinbayparasail.com

There are many other things to see and do on the islands. If you are planning to spend the night or a few days, contact:

Put-in-Bay Visitors & Convention Bureau
www.putinbay.com • 888-742-7829

Underground Ohio

Put-in-Bay

While you might not expect it, Ohio has a large number of underground caves that are open for exploration. The most famous are the Ohio Caverns in West Liberty, Olentangy Caverns near Columbus, Zane Shawnee Caverns near Bellefontaine, and Seneca Caverns near Bellevue.

Over the years, I have visited all of them, despite the fact that I suffer from claustrophobia and usually can't wait to get back above ground. But, hey, it's part of the job.

If I had to choose a favorite cave on the basis of ease of entry, minimal amount of walking required, and level of interest, it would probably be the **Crystal Cave** on South Bass Island in Lake Erie.

Just the fact that a cave is on an island and you can only get there by boat or airplane makes this destination really unique. But, as they say on TV, "Wait! There's more!" Crystal Cave is a limestone cave that is actually lined with natural crystals.

In 1897, Gustav Heineman, a German immigrant, came to the island and started a winery bearing his name. He needed a well and hired some workmen to dig one, using picks and shovels. When they reached a depth of about 30 feet beneath the winery, they struck a vug, or cavity, in the limestone, and discovered it was filled with crystals.

Analysis of the large, tabular crystals revealed that they were celestine, a form of strontium sulfate used for making fireworks. For a while, Heineman mined and sold the crystals. Then one day, he realized that instead of mining, he might make more money by turning the cave into a tourist attraction. He was right.

What he had was one of the largest geodes in the world. A geode is a rock with crystals inside. The cave was an instant hit with tourists and, in fact, became an economic life saver for the Heineman family when Prohibition was enacted in 1919, stopping the sale of wine. The sale of grape juice and admission to the crystal cave kept the winery going during the 1920s until Prohibition was finally repealed in the early 1930s.

The tour of the cave doesn't take very long. You walk down about

Crystal Cave, owned by the Heinemann Winery, has been an island attraction for generations.

40 steps to the bottom of the cave floor. No matter what time of year it is, the temperature is always about 60 degrees in the cave. Specially placed lights illuminate the crystals clinging to the walls and ceiling of the passageway, which was carved through the crystals. The tour circles through the crystal and ends back at the stairway. A guide gives a short history of the cave and how it was found, and can usually answer most questions.

Today, you can combine a tour of the cave with a walk through the winery and see how the wine is produced. You'll end your visit with a complimentary glass of wine or grape juice in the garden at the back of the winery.

Heineman Winery and Crystal Cave
978 Catawba Ave • Put-in-Bay, South Bass Island, OH   419-285-2811
www.heinemanswinery.com

For more ideas in the area, see other chapters in this book or:

Put-in-Bay Chamber of Commerce
www.visitputinbay.com • 419-285-2832

Skimming Sandusky Bay

Sandusky

Picture this. You're in a boat in water sometimes less than a foot deep and you are traveling at speeds of 40 to 50 miles per hour. On the shore, the outline of the Cedar Point Amusement Park is a blur. No, it's not some new Cedar Point thrill ride. You are a passenger in an airboat.

Just outside Cedar Point in the marshy part of Sandusky Bay on the east side of the Cedar Point Causeway, **Air 1 Airboats** of Sandusky offers speed and thrills.

Capt. Tony Muscioni, the owner, is a licensed Lake Erie fishing guide. For years, he has used the powerful, nimble, flat-bottomed airboats to take ice fishermen miles out onto frozen Lake Erie in the winter. However, during the hot summer months, his airboats were unused. Realizing that in tropical climates, airboat rides through swamps were a big tourist attraction, Tony decided to see whether they might be equally popular in the shallow parts of Sandusky Bay.

They have. Hundreds of families have taken the one-of-a-kind ride that circles and crisscrosses a shallow marsh between the two roads leading to the Cedar Point Peninsula.

The boats can carry up to six people. You board the craft at a small marina on River Avenue, just off Cedar Point Drive, the main road to the amusement park.

Each passenger is given a set of noise-cancelling headphones to wear. Remember, you are sitting just a few feet in front of a large engine and propeller that make a lot of noise.

Captain Tony sits in a tall chair in the center of the rear of the boat where the controls are, and the passengers sit lower in the front of the craft. The noise level isn't bad as the boat slowly leaves the dock and cruises past beautiful bayfront homes. However, when it reaches the edge of the marshy bay, the fun begins.

The engine roars to full throttle and the boat starts skimming across the water, faster and faster, almost flying, at speeds of nearly 50 miles per hour.

On a hot summer day with the wind and spray in your face, you might see flocks of low-flying geese you almost seem to be racing across the water. You roar past lines of traffic slowly inching their way to the amusement park parking lot and skim over lily pads glistening in the sun.

The boat is driven by the airplane-type propeller that uses air to push you along. When under full power, the boat barely touches the surface of the bay. Unlike a regular boat, there is no wheel for steering; instead, the captain uses an airplane-like rudder stick to direct the craft. Sometimes Captain Tony lets guests take over the stick under his watchful eye.

Each ride last 30 to 40 minutes. In those minutes, you will see beautiful homes, great scenery, a view of Sandusky Bay that can only be seen from a boat, and, most important, you'll feel the thrill of a high speed run across shimmering water. It's an experience the whole family can enjoy and take away as a special memory.

Air 1 Airboats
2312 River Ave • Sandusky, OH   419-366-8472
www.air1airboats.com

For more ideas in the area:

Lake Erie Shores and Islands
www.shoresandislands.com • 419-625-2984

Ice Fishing on Lake Erie

Sandusky

Winter on Lake Erie.

Cold. Isolation. Majestic. Other-worldly.

All of these words apply to ice fishing on Lake Erie in February.

Even if you are not a fisherman, I would still recommend you try it, just for the adventure. I did.

My day began at 3:00 a.m. I dressed in layers. Two pairs of warm pants over thermal underwear. A wool shirt, topped by a warm sweater, all of this under my winter parka. And a pair of thermal boots.

I was ready to go ice fishing.

We met Captain Tony Muscioni at 6:00 a.m. in the parking lot of the West Catawba State Park, near Port Clinton.

He loaded us aboard his airboat, fired up the motor, and we drove down a ramp onto the rugged ice of Lake Erie.

A word about riding in airboats across a frozen lake: While it is warm and comfortable in the enclosed cabin, all you hear is the roar of the giant airplane-like propeller behind you as you travel over the ice. The ride is rough. If you have ever gone four-wheeling through rough terrain, you'll recognize airboating over the wind-blown chunks of ice as a close cousin. The difference is that on the airboat, there are no seatbelts to keep you in your seat when the boat leaps over an outcropping of ice and slams back onto the surface of the lake.

Once away from the shore, we reached patches of smoother ice and the speed increased. It took about 45 minutes for Captain Tony to maneuver us nearly four miles out on the frozen lake to a place his experience has shown plenty of fish will be biting.

When he turned off the motor, the roar of the turning propeller was replaced by a sudden silence broken only by the whisper of the wind whipping curtains of snow crystals across the frozen surface.

It was a gray morning, and no sun peeked through the clouds. No horizon could be seen in any direction, just white nothingness. The wind and the snow obliterated distant landmarks on the shore. There was a sense of isolation, perhaps what the arctic explorers might feel.

As we stepped out of the heated cabin on the airboat, all the poetry

About four miles from shore, my Fox 8 TV crew watches Capt. Tony drill through the ice in preparation for ice-fishing. *(Tomi Toyama-Ambrose)*

and majesty of the white landscape disappeared as we felt the cold biting, aching, burning any bit of exposed skin.

Out on the ice, it was five below zero and with the wind, unhampered by trees and buildings, the wind-chill factor made it feel even colder.

Captain Tony seemed oblivious to the cold, and immediately went to work hauling a gas-powered auger from the boat and started drilling holes through the nearly two-foot-thick ice. He set up a small frame around each hole, then stretched a plastic covering over the frame, creating what, from a distance, could be mistaken for a porta-potty. The little plastic structure gives the fisherman a respite from the wind. With the help of a small kerosene heater, we were ready to fish.

Because I did not have a fishing license, I was not participating. But one of the fishermen on the trip caught a walleye so big, he could hardly get it through the hole in the ice. It turned out to weigh nearly 15 pounds.

When the wind dropped, we could see other, similar fishing shacks dotting the ice, perhaps a half-mile away. It was almost magical, as the village of fishermen would be there one moment and, with a gust of wind, disappear into a wall of white. In the distance, we could also see fishermen arriving and departing on snowmobiles and small ATVs.

Considering how far out on the lake we were, I felt much safer in an airboat, which can travel over ice or water.

By lunchtime, the sun had popped out, and although the temperature was still near zero, it felt warm on our faces.

Inside the fishing shack, sandwiches and soft drinks appeared from a cooler that Captain Tony had brought. The fishermen were still busy, and a small pile of fish grew on the ice nearby. No cooler was needed to store your catch out here.

At 2:00 p.m., Captain Tony started taking down the fishing shacks and putting them back in the boat. The holes that had been used for fishing had already started to freeze shut. We picked up our scraps and plastic bottles, put them in a garbage bag, and boarded the airboat for the trip back to the mainland.

As I said, even if you don't like to fish, this is a once-in-a-lifetime adventure to see Lake Erie from a unique perspective. A sort of one-of-kind One Tank Trip.

Air 1 Airboats
2312 River Ave • Sandusky, OH   419-366-8472
www.icefishinglakeerie.com

Even in the dead of winter, there are many things to do in the Sandusky Bay-Lake Erie Island area. See other chapters in this book for ideas or contact:

Lake Erie Shores & Islands Welcome Center
www.shoresandislands.com • 419-625-2984

For a Rainy Day

Port Clinton, Put-in-Bay, Sandusky

We've all had it happen. We plan for weeks for a vacation or holiday and when the week arrives, so does the worst weather of the year. It's difficult to enjoy places like Cedar Point or even the Lake Erie Islands in a day-long downpour. Over the years, we have faced the same problems with One Tank Trips. This is how we've saved the day and made some fun discoveries.

There are several indoor attractions in the Sandusky Bay area.

One that immediately comes to mind is the **Merry-Go-Round Museum** in downtown Sandusky. Formerly a U.S. Post Office building, the museum opened in 1990 and has a full sized, working carousel in the center of the building. The horses and figures on the carousel are part of the museum's collection, and reflect hundreds of years of carousel history. Visitors can ride on the carousel and see how the horses or other figures are carved. There is a small gift shop where you can buy souvenirs as well as carousel music.

Another rainy day destination is the **Liberty Aviation Museum** in Port Clinton. It is home to a World War II B-25 bomber and assorted other war birds as well as tanks, ambulances and jeeps from that period. They also are restoring a World War II-era PT boat that will be used to give rides to visitors on Lake Erie when it's completed.

This unique museum has another attraction, an operating 1950s diner, where the proceeds from food sales are used to help operate the museum. The Tin Goose Diner offers really good food, and don't forget to try the milkshakes.

Speaking of the Tin Goose, Liberty Aviation Museum also owns *The City of Port Clinton,* one of the last flying Ford Tri-Motor airplanes that were fondly called "Tin Goose" because of their corrugated metal construction. *The City of Port Clinton* frequently tours the country, but is home at the museum several times each year. In addition, another Ford Tri-Motor aircraft is being rebuilt by volunteers inside the museum, and you can watch their progress when you visit.

Liberty Aviation Museum is on the grounds of the Erie-Ottawa International Airport that was once home to Island Airlines, the

"World's Shortest Airline." Ford Tri-Motors were used to fly folks to the Lake Erie Islands, a flight that took about five minutes.

By the way, even in bad weather, you can usually get to the islands on the ferry from Catawba Island. Over the years, I have made the crossing to the islands many times in all kinds of weather on the **Miller Boat Line**. Truth be told, I enjoy doing it on windy days when the boat is plunging up and down in the waves. It's kind of like taking a roller coaster ride at Cedar Point.

Once on the islands, there are lots of things to do, even in the rain. The Lake Erie Islands Historical Society has a wonderful museum in Put-in-Bay where exhibits trace the history of the island and the people who have come here for recreation. The Perry's Victory and International Peace Memorial has a great visitors center that explains the War of 1812 and the Battle of Lake Erie, and admission is free.

A rainy day doesn't have to mean the fun stops.

Merry Go Round Museum
301 Jackson St • Sandusky, OH   419-626-6111
www.merrygoroundmuseum.org

Liberty Aviation Museum
3515 E State Rd • Port Clinton, OH   419-732-0234
www.libertyaviationmuseum.org

Miller Boat Line
535 Bayview Ave • Put-in-Bay, OH   800-500-2421
www.millerferry.com

I enjoy riding the Ferry even in wet weather. *(Miller Boat Line)*

Live Your Racing Fantasy in the Family Car

Norwalk

Huron County is one of a number of mostly rural counties in northern Ohio. It's a place of farms and small towns with tree-shaded streets. The Firelands Museum in Norwalk is one of Ohio's oldest museums. But Norwalk also has another attraction that brings thousands of visitors to this community each year.

Do you want something to get your adrenalin pumping? To hear the howling thunder of automobile motors pushed to their limits? To smell the smoke of burning rubber? How about taking the family car out to a racetrack where you can put the pedal to the metal and see just how fast the old jalopy can really go. You don't have to have any racing experience; just a driver's license. You race against the clock or another driver who is also living his or her fantasy.

Summit Motorsports Park in Norwalk is home to the National Hot Rod Association (NHRA), where such names as John Force, Cruz Pedregon and Ron Capps pack the racetrack's 38,000 seats several times a year.

Normally, the Park hosts bracket racing or other special events such as Pontiac Weekend, Fords at the Summit Weekend, The Blue Suede Cruise, and the popular annual Night Under Fire. But since 1975, they have also dedicated selected dates each year, usually on Wednesdays, to allow racing fans and wannabe race drivers to use the track to race just about anything they drive, from home-built racers and motorcycles to the family car or truck.

On those nights, it is not unusual to find a professional, nationally-ranked hot rod racer at the track, testing a new engine or setting his clutch side-by-side with a family getting ready to check out the performance of the four-door sedan that normally carries their kids to school.

NHRA president Bill Bader Jr. told me the Wednesday night open track allows anyone who has ever thought about racing a chance to try some hands-on basics of the sport without spending a lot of money.

This is the way it works: If you have a car, truck, or motorcycle that

Bill Bader, Sr., an iconic figure in drag racing, chats with one of the many non-professional drivers on a Wednesday night at the Summit Motor Sports Park.

you think is fast, but don't want to risk a speeding ticket to find out just how fast, head over to the Summit Motorsports Park on selected Wednesday evenings from late April through the end of September. From 5:30 p.m. to 8:30 p.m., they run time trials. There is a modest fee to either race or just watch.

Once you are inside the facility, you get in line with the other 200 or 300 people who have come to run their cars. The line moves pretty quickly. You are waved onto the track, where you are given a few seconds to drive into the water box and wet your tires. (The purpose is to wet the tires and spin them to a high speed to heat them, which allows them to grip the pavement and achieve better traction.) Next, you pull up to a stanchion with a series of lights known as the "Christmas tree." When the lights change from yellow to green, you punch the accelerator and hurl down the quarter-mile track. How fast you go is up to your driving ability, your vehicle's capabilities, and your courage.

When you finish your run and circle back, a timekeeper will hand you a slip that has the lapsed time and miles-per-hour that you achieved at the finish line. If you want to go again, you can get in line and, depending on the crowd, you can probably get a second run in before 8:30 p.m., when the racing starts.

At that time, the announcer will call out several groups of racers who will then compete in various categories, based on their speed, and ranging from family cars, trucks, and motorcycles to vehicles built strictly for racing. The winners receive trophies and the highest-rated drivers move on to a race later in the year with a grand prize of several thousand dollars.

Like many racing parks, the concession area offers all kinds of racing memorabilia, but there is one store at the track that hasn't changed over time. They have a tradition here that dates back more than 30 years. For $1, you get a large styrofoam cup packed with not just a dip or two, but one full pound of Toft's ice cream. That's right: an entire pound. The price hasn't changed in three decades.

The Summit Motorsports Park
1300 State Rte 18 • Norwalk, OH   419-668-5555
www.norwalkraceway.com

If you are planning to stay overnight, check the local tourism and convention bureau for other attractions and places to stay.

Visit Huron County
www.visithuroncounty.com • 419-668-4155

Bird-Watching on Lake Erie

Oak Harbor

If you long to gaze at the ruby-crowned kinglets or a palm warbler then you want to set your destination for an area along Lake Erie between Toledo and Port Clinton.

Some call this the warbler capital of the U.S.

Each May, thousands and thousands of bird watchers from all over the world crowd the **Magee Marsh Wildlife Area** and other bird sanctuaries along the south shore of Lake Erie to watch the miracle of migration as millions of small and large birds stop here on their journey to their breeding grounds in Canada across Lake Erie.

Scientists believe that the birds rest in the marshy groves that creep into the lake along the shore before starting the long flight over water. The migration starts each year in April with the arrival of palm warblers, ruby-crowned kinglets, myrtle warblers, and gnatcatchers. It reaches a crescendo in mid-May, when at least a dozen and a half other breeds of warblers join the gathering. This does not include all the other types of birds passing through or settling in to spend the summer on Lake Erie.

I confess, I have never had much interest in bird watching, but after seeing the turnout one spring at Magee Marsh, I have a new appreciation and respect for the hobby.

The Marsh covers almost 2,000 acres of Lake Erie shoreline owned by the Division of Wildlife—Ohio Department of Natural Resources.

More than 300 species of birds pass through Magee Marsh each year, but what brings out the birders and their cameras and notebooks are the 30-plus breeds of warbler seen here each spring.

In the third week of May, an estimated 50,000 people crowd the observation deck, trails, and roadways of the marsh, scanning the sky, bushes, trees, and fields for a glimpse of a yellow-rumped warbler or the rare Kirtland's warbler, a tiny bird with black stripes down his sides and bearing a yellow throat, breast, and belly.

Bird watchers are a friendly crowd. At least, that is what I experienced the day I spent at Magee Marsh in May. People from five states and a couple from Germany introduced themselves to me and after realizing I was a novice, pointed out birds in trees and bushes that I had missed. They willingly shared bird identification books.

On my visit, it wasn't just warblers that I saw. There were magnificent trumpeter swans, snowy egrets, and cranes standing on one leg in a still pond. We also saw deer, woodchuck, and even a skunk, which, thankfully, was waddling away from us.

Even if the weather turns windy or rain should dampen the search for birds, at the Sportsman Migratory Bird Center, you can pick up a map, get a bird checklist and—this is important—find restrooms with running water.

The Sportsman Migratory Bird Center also has an amazing mounted display of almost every kind of bird, animal and fish you will find in the marsh. It is a great way to get an up-close look at some of the rarer species in a dry and comfortable setting.

Admission to the marsh is free. Best of all bird watching is something that just about every member of the family can participate in.

Magee Marsh Wildlife Area
13229 W State Rte 2 • Oak Harbor, OH   419-898-0960
www.friendsofmageemarsh.org

For other things to do in the area, contact:

Lake Erie Shores and Islands
www.shoresandislands.com • 419-625-2984

The Sportsman Migratory Bird Center at Magee Marsh.

Ohio's Caviest Cave

Bellevue

The **Seneca Caverns** near Bellevue, named one of Ohio's Natural Landmarks by former Gov. George Voinovich, is perhaps the most "natural" commercial cave in the state and one of the most unusual in the country.

It has been called the "Caviest Cave in America."

The caverns in the flat farmland of northwestern Ohio were discovered in 1872 by two farm boys who were out hunting. Originally known as Good's Cave, it was named for the family that owned the farm where the discovery was made. For years it was just a local curiosity. That all changed in 1929, when attorney Don Bell got involved.

Bell saw the possibility of turning the caverns into a tourist attraction, and after purchasing the site, he set to work, bucket by bucket, cleaning out the glacial clay-packed caverns and discovered it was larger than originally believed. It took more than two years of back-breaking labor to excavate mud and rubble from the chambers, but it was finally opened it to tourists in 1933. Bell also changed the name of the caverns to "Seneca" to honor the Native Americans who had once lived just west of the caverns.

Two generations of the Bell family have operated Seneca Caverns for more than 80 years.

The caverns have existed for thousands, and perhaps millions of years. It's believed they were created by an underground river that flooded, pushing water through the soil and rock beneath the ground, washing the softer material, gypsum, away and allowing the limestone that was left to collapse, leaving underground chambers.

Don Bell's son Rich and his wife Denise eventually took over operation of the caverns.

Rich, a geological engineer, said the caverns go down seven levels to a depth of 110 feet, where an underground river flows north into the Blue Hole in Castalia and Lake Erie.

This is not your average commercial cave with even steps and smooth walkways. It was intentionally left as natural as possible. Visitors have to step over rock outcroppings and duck under and squeeze

Seneca Caverns.

through some openings. Steps carved out of the stone are functional, but uneven.

The guided tours usually last about an hour. Most healthy people can handle the tour, but the Bells suggest that, because of the natural makeup of the cave, those who have physical problems and would have problems walking or climbing steps or are claustrophobic might want to wait in the gift shop while others take the tour.

There are only a few mineral growths in the caverns. Rich Bell said he and other geologists aren't sure why. There are theories that the rock forming the caves is too porous and doesn't allow the slow formation of stalactites or it could be that the caves are just not old enough.

Because of the ebb and flow of the underground river, especially in springtime, the lower levels are sometimes flooded and are not open to tours.

In the first and second levels, you can see graffiti such as names and initials carved in the rock by early explorers to the cave more than a century ago.

Fossils are embedded in the limestone cavern walls. On the third level, there is a rare fossil from the time a huge sea covered this area, a Devonian armored fish.

For those who want more than to explore a cave, there is another attraction on the site—gemstone mining. It consists of a water sluice where, for a price, you can buy a bag of "tailings," cast-off dirt and stones from mines all over the world, that you swish through a screened box in the sluice water to search for emeralds, arrowheads, and fossils. Each bag is guaranteed to have something of value.

Rich Bell grew up in the caverns and even in his eighties, was still training tour guides and leading occasional tours, especially high school earth science classes or groups of professional geologists.

Sadly, Rich Bell passed away in 2011. His wife Denise, with the help of family members, still operates the caverns today.

Seneca Caverns
15248 E Thompson Rd • Bellevue, OH   419-483-6711
www.senecacavernsohio.com

For more ideas in the area, see other chapters in this book or:

Bellevue Area Tourism and Visitor Bureau
www.bellevuetourism.org • 419-684-4030

Digging Ohio's Prehistoric Past

Sylvania

One of the most unique city-owned parks in Ohio is located in Sylvania in the northwest corner of the state.

Some 375 million years ago, during the Devonian period, Ohio was on the bottom of a prehistoric sea. That enormous ocean was filled with all kinds of living things. Fast forward to the Sylvania of today, which is located on one of only two prime Devonian-era sites in the entire world. The other is in France. The Devonian era is so-named because fossils from that period were first found and studied in Devon, England.

What does all that mean? It means there is a park in Sylvania where you can barely turn over a rock without finding some kind of fossil. And here is the best part: What you find is yours to keep.

Fossil Park, a city-owned park in the Olander Park System, is a five-acre abandoned stone quarry.

You walk down a graded walk to the bottom of the quarry hole. Because shovels and tools are not allowed in the park, you use just your hands to chip and pry apart the soft, gray, flaky shale in the hope of finding trilobites, which look something like a prehistoric beetle; brachiopods, which were shell-like creatures; horn coral, which resemble small ice cream cones; and crinoids, often called sea lilies.

The shale containing the fossils is actually trucked into Fossil Park from a nearby working quarry. It would be too dangerous to allow fossil hunters into the active quarry.

To identify any finds, there are usually park volunteers on hand during regular hours, as well as large information boards with pictures of the various fossils.

The day we visited, a group of school children were going through piles of shale. It was only minutes until they started to find some brachiopods, which appear to be the most common fossil here. Most of the discoveries that morning were just bits and pieces of fossils, but several complete specimens also were discovered.

While these millions-of-years-old fossils are fairly common, they do have value. A check of online auction sites revealed many such

Digging for fossils at Fossil Park, located in an abandoned stone quarry.

specimens for sale at prices ranging from a couple of dollars all the way up to $30 or $40.

There are modern restrooms and water fountains in the parking lot at the top of the quarry hole.

Fossil hunting is seasonal. The quarry pit is open from April to November, and admission is free.

Be sure to bring along a brush to clean up the fossils you find and a bag to carry your finds home.

Fossil Park
5705 Centennial Rd • Sylvania, OH   419-882-8313
www.olanderpark.com

For more ideas in the area, see other chapters in this book or:

Destination Toledo
www.dotoledo.org • 419-321-6404

National Museum of the Great Lakes

Toledo

The **National Museum of the Great Lakes** opened in 2014 along the Maumee River in a building that the city of Toledo had hoped would become a terminal for a Canadian ferryboat service and passenger boats. That didn't happen.

The old Great Lakes Museum was located for many years in Vermilion. The new building here in Toledo is about four times larger and offers so much more than could be displayed at the former location.

It has four themed areas. One covers the exploration and settlement of the Great Lakes. Another, Shipwrecks and Survival, notes that there are more than 8,000 shipwrecks scattered across the bottom of the five lakes: Huron, Superior, Michigan, Erie, and Ontario. You can see a lifeboat from the most famous Great Lakes shipwreck, the *Edmund Fitzgerald*. Visitors will also enjoy a computer simulated diving bell that allows you to direct a submerged search of the sunken ship.

Lake history abounds here. You can see pieces of Oliver Hazard Perry's brig *Niagara* from the War of 1812. There is crockery and dinnerware from the age of cruise ships that once carried passengers from city to city on the Great Lakes. You will also learn that during World War II, the navy built an aircraft carrier out of old cruise ships and trained navy flyers on the lakes.

In all, there are about 250 nautical items on display that fill nearly 6,000 square feet in the Maritime Building. And, according to a spokesperson, that only represents about 10 to 15 percent of the total number of artifacts owned by the NGLM. Items will be rotated as often as possible to keep the museum fresh and interesting.

But not all the exhibits are inside the building.

The largest single artifact is the lake freighter *Col. James M. Schoonmaker*. At 600 feet in length the *Schoonmaker* was the biggest ship operating on the Great Lakes for a time after it was launched in 1913. It hauled freight through most of the twentieth century before being retired. The ship's interior is still being slowly restored to its original appearance.

In fact, the museum buildings, grounds and outside exhibits are

A drone's-eye view of the National Museum of the Great Lakes. *(Shawn Rames)*

so huge that they are best seen from the air. The day we visited, we were lucky enough to meet Shawn Rames, a man with a passion for photography and radio-controlled drones that enabled him to get some unique and unusual shots of both the *Schoonmaker*, and the courtyard sculpture of the entire Great Lakes.

Rames was kind enough to give us copies of his video, which we incorporated into our One Tank Trip, allowing us to show aerial shots of the *Schoonmaker* from the front to the back of the 600-foot ship. He closed with a shot of Rames and me standing on the sidewalk by the museum, then flew the drone up several hundred feet until he and I were just dots on the sidewalk and you could see the entire museum and ship at dock.

In my earlier years in television, a shot like that would have required a helicopter, a pilot, and a photographer, and would have cost thousands of dollars to make.

National Museum of the Great Lakes
1701 Front St • Toledo, OH   419-214-5000
www.inlandseas.org

For more ideas in Toledo, see:

Destination Toledo
www.dotoledo.org • 419-321-640

SOUTHWEST OHIO

Shopping in the Jungle

Fairfield

Who would ever dream that a trip to the grocery store could become a fun destination for a One Tank Trip? **Jungle Jim's International Market** in Southwest Ohio is anything but your everyday grocery.

How to start?

Well, for openers, this might be the only food market that has a real antique fire truck inside the store hovering over 1,000 different kinds of hot sauce. Would you believe that there is a 45-foot-long yacht anchored in the seafood department? A cheese counter with more than 1,600 varieties of cheese? The fresh produce area fills a space larger than some supermarkets, and could serve as an example of a vegetable stand in the Garden of Eden, with exotic fruits and vegetables from every part of the Earth.

The store is so massive that they offer maps of the building at the front entrance. They even have a guide available for tours. Many people come from three states to just look, but most also come to buy. Jungle Jim refers to his customers as "foodies." The entrance to this "foodie" paradise has its own waterfall, pond and life-size fiberglass animals, such as elephants and giant birds, grazing amid manmade palm trees.

Owner James Bonaminio, aka "Jungle Jim," is a grocer on steroids. Everything about his market is big and over the top. The store alone

A monorail once used at Kings Island Amusement Park now carries guests to the Oscar Center above Jungle Jim's Marketplace.

covers a staggering six acres and sits in the middle of more than 70 acres of choice realty along busy U.S. Route 4, the Dixie Highway, in Butler County and north of Cincinnati.

"Different" is the operative word here. In many grocery stores, the public restrooms are usually predictable: places you only want to visit in extreme emergencies. Jungle Jim encourages his customers to at least look at his restrooms, even if you don't want to use the facilities. He won an award for the best public restrooms in America. One will give you a chuckle: The doorway is a porta-potty that really serves as the entrance to a large, well-equipped, clean restroom. Another bathroom in the complex can only be described as luxurious, with marble floors, chandeliers, velvet sofas, paintings, and palms.

Also, how many grocers do you know who zip up and down the aisles of their store on a Segway, the two-wheeled personal transporter of the twenty-first century? And the costumes: Bonaminio has been known to stroll through the store wearing his trademark pith helmet and bush jacket or dressed as a cowboy, a fireman, and even a wizard. When he was inducted into the Ohio Grocers Hall of Fame, he surprised the audience by accepting the award dressed head-to-toe in gold Middle Eastern garb, complete with a turban.

Bonaminio was born in Lorain. He began his career in food marketing while attending college in Southwest Ohio. His career in grocery started with a roadside vegetable stand not far from where his sprawling complex stands today. Bonaminio's innovative, and sometimes wacky marketing ideas have not only attracted customers, but allowed his business to expand again and again. He recently opened another giant store, taking over a troubled strip mall on the east side of Cincinnati near the Eastgate Shopping Center.

As you stroll through the labyrinth of aisles, you will find long rows dedicated to canned, frozen, and fresh foods from 75 different countries and cultures. In many of the departments, there are kiosks with free samples. Tucked away in one corner of the store is a small theater, where a movie depicting the history of Jungle Jim's International Market runs continuously. In another spot, a life-size, singing, animated lion dressed as Elvis periodically entertains passing customers.

Jungle Jim's has a bank, a pharmacy, a garden center and even a U.S. Post Office.

Want to have your wedding in a beautiful place? How about one with a winding stairway, a lobby with a grand piano and antique fixtures, where you can make a dramatic arrival by monorail? You can do it at the Oscar. Oscar is Bonaminio's middle name, and it's the name he gave the 1,200-seat event center incorporated into his mega-store. You can reach it by steps from the ground floor or you can drive to the monorail station at the rear of the property and take a futuristic ride that once was a popular attraction at King's Island Amusement Park. The ride will take you across the parking lot and around the building to deposit you at the second-level entrance to the Oscar Event Center. You just don't find attractions like this at your corner grocery store.

Bonaminio has attracted much national attention over the last several years for his unorthodox approach to grocery marketing. With more than 50,000 people per week passing through his stores, he sums it up this way: "This is a serious business. I'm here to make money." Then he adds with a smile, "But no one said you can't have fun along the way."

Jungle Jim's International Market
5440 Dixie Hwy • Fairfield, OH   513-674-6000
www.junglejims.com

For more in the area, see other chapters in this book or:

CincinnatiUSA Convention & Visitors Bureau
859-581-2260
www.cincinnatiusa.com

A Place to Join the Circus

Cincinnati

Have you ever dreamed of running away to join the circus? Fantasized about being the man or woman on the high trapeze? Envied those stilt-walking clowns and jugglers?

We found a circus school in Cincinnati that can teach you to do all those things, even if you don't want to join the circus.

David Willacker, a juggler, started to turn his hobby into a business in 2005, when he and some friends converted their abilities to juggle, stilt-walk, and paint faces into "The Amazing Portable Circus" that traveled around the city giving programs to kids and schools.

It was successful, so they kept adding circus-type acts, such as making balloon animals and fire-eating. But it was in 2010, when David brought the first flying trapeze to Ohio and they became The **Cincinnati Circus Company**, that their popularity really soared.

It now meant just about anyone could try his hand at sailing through the air while clutching onto a real flying trapeze.

The trapeze rig is just like the ones used in big circuses, except there is no big top. The trapeze is set up in Burnet Woods Park, just a short walk from the University of Cincinnati's main campus.

The Cincinnati Circus Company offers daily lessons on the trapeze for experienced aerialists, but, for a nominal fee, they also will let just about anyone who is strong enough and can hold his own body weight while hanging from a bar, to have a trapeze experience.

First, there is ground school with an instructor who explains the timing and how the trapeze works. Then he or she fits you into a flyer's harness and explains the safety issues involved, and you are ready.

You just have to scamper up a small ladder about 30 feet in the air, stand on a narrow platform while wearing a harness with safety ropes attached, grab a trapeze bar that an instructor catches for you, and then, when the moment is just right and with the instructor's lessons still in your ears, you step off into space and for a moment, you are flying as you swing across a safety net spread beneath you.

Depending on your skill level, you might attempt to swing out and grab another trapeze bar. Others may just swing out and back while

A first flight on the flying trapese: standing high above the ground in the rigging, waiting to take off.

hanging by their legs, or, as most customers do on their first time, just hang on for dear life and swing back and forth 20 or so feet in the air until your arms start to ache.

When you are done, the instructor orders you to release the trapeze and you drop into the net below. It is truly an experience you won't soon forget.

Scouts, church groups, and families all come here for this once-in-a-lifetime thrill.

Because it is located outdoors, the trapeze is a seasonal event. The Cincinnati Circus Company offers instruction in other circus skills year-round at their various indoor facilities.

Cincinnati Circus Company
6433 Wiehe Rd • Cincinnati, OH   513-921-5454
www.cincinnaticircus.com

For more in the Cincinnati area, see other chapters of this book, or:

Cincinnati USA Convention & Visitors Bureau
www.cincinnatiusa.com • 513-621-2142

An Ohio Icon, Clifton Mill

Clifton

Grist mills, those water-powered mills that early Ohio settlers used to grind their corn and grain into flour, always seem to be located in bucolic locations. If I had to select the most iconic mill in the Buckeye State, it would be **Clifton Mill**.

It's located in Greene County, just outside the tiny town of Yellow Springs. A mill has been operating on this site since 1802. In fact, corn was ground here to feed American troops during the War of 1812.

Today, Clifton Mill is one of the oldest and largest water-powered mills still in existence. The water comes from the Little Miami River. The mill is situated on the Clifton Gorge, part of a two-mile-long stretch of the Little Miami, which is both a state and a national scenic river and contains some of the most impressive dolomite and lime-stone cliffs to be found in the country.

The latest owners of the mill, the Satariano family, restored the mill and made it the tourist destination that it is today. They added a small restaurant overlooking the gorge and a nearby covered bridge. On the menu are pancakes, huge pancakes made with meal ground in their own mill. Pancakes so big, they fill a plate, leaving no room for syrup and butter. In fact, to eat them, you have to cut a small hole in the center to put the syrup, otherwise it pours off the pancakes onto the table. I dubbed them "manhole" pancakes.

Spring, summer, and autumn are great times to visit the mill. In the spring, the gorge is filled with wildflowers and the spring rains increase the flow that roars through the gorge. In the summertime, you can see the mill in action and stroll for miles along the scenic river. Autumn, and the gorge is painted in changing leaf colors. This is one of my favorite places to see autumn in Ohio.

But it is Christmastime when the mill really shines. That is when the Satariano family covers the historic building in lights. They spread a carpet of colored lights over a nearby cliff, creating a waterfall of moving lights that reflects in the Little Miami River below. A miniature town of Clifton is created by the millstream with lights and animated figures that stage a Christmas parade every few minutes. In all, more

Clifton Mill, one of the largest water-powered gristmills still operating.

than 3.5 million colored lights illuminate the mill and nearby gorge.

A building on the grounds becomes Santa's workshop, and a live Santa can be seen through the windows, working on toys. Every 15 minutes, he goes to a fireplace and, moments later, appears on the roof, chatting with youngsters on the ground below.

The lights are turned on each year on the night after Thanksgiving and are on every night until December 31. There is an admission fee to the mill and grounds during the holiday season.

The Satarianos often ask local celebrities to be the "illuminator" who flips the single switch that turns on all of the lights. Over the years, my granddaughter Allison McCallister and I have had the honor of twice being asked to start the mill's holiday season by throwing the switch.

Clifton Mill is a great year-round family destination.

Clifton Mill
75 Water St • Clifton, OH   937-767-5501
www.cliftonmill.com

For more in the Dayton-Xenia area, see other chapters in this book or:

Greene County Convention & Visitors Bureau
www.greenecountyohio.org • 937-429-9100

Ohio's Best Free Attraction

Dayton

Now, understand when I say, "best free attraction," I am stating an opinion. It is my opinion, and you have every right not to agree with me. However, I think you will be hard pressed to find another tourist destination in our state that offers so much, for so little.

I am speaking of the **National Museum of the United States Air Force** at Wright-Patterson Air Force Base in Dayton, Ohio.

You can't beat the price. Admission is free.

The museum consists of some of the most famous aircraft in the world, beginning with some of the early aircraft made by Orville and Wilbur Wright all the way up through space capsules used in our journey to the moon.

Inside and out at the series of giant hangers that store the historic aircraft, there are things to see. From a World War II control tower and Nissen huts to modern day aircraft taking off and landing at nearby Wright-Patterson air fields.

Perhaps the gem of the site is the museum hangar that houses the presidential aircraft. Here you will find John F. Kennedy's Air Force One, the Boeing 707, known as SAM (Special Air Mission) 26000. This is the plane Kennedy flew to Dallas on the day he was assassinated and the plane that carried his body back to Washington, D.C.

That same aircraft holds another historic distinction. It was the where Lyndon B. Johnson was sworn in as president following Kennedy's death. It went on to serve other presidents through the administration of Bill Clinton.

The gallery contains other aircraft associated with presidents in the twentieth century, including the very first presidential plane, known as the "Sacred Cow," a Douglas VC-54C used by Franklin Delano Roosevelt. It is fitted with a custom elevator because he had polio and was unable to walk.

The name "Air Force One" applies to any aircraft that the president happens to be flying in, and the museum has several small craft used by various presidents for short hops that were, at the time, also referred to as "Air Force One."

Presidential aircraft on display at the National Museum of the United States Air Force.

One of my favorites of these is a U-4B, or a twin-engine Aero Commander that Dwight D. Eisenhower used to go from Washington to his farm in Gettysburg, Pennsylvania. It's a little-known fact, but while serving under Gen. Douglas MacArthur in the Philippines prior to World War II, Eisenhower took flying lessons. While president, he often took the controls during his frequent flights to Gettysburg.

Although admission to the main museum is free, you can spend some money. There is a large 3-D museum theater that presents a variety of documentaries and other types of movies. You'll pay an admission fee for the movie. There is also a wonderful museum store, where you will need some money to take home books and souvenirs.

Other than that, this is definitely one of the best, if not *the* best free attraction in Ohio.

National Museum of the United States Air Force
Wright Patterson Air Force Base • 1100 Spaatz St, Dayton OH   937-255-3286
www.nationalmuseum.af.mil

For more ideas in the area, contact:

Greene County Convention and Visitors Bureau
www.greenecountyohio.org • 937-429-9100

Fly With Bugs in Your Teeth

Miamisburg

I like trips that have a rare, one-of-a-kind destination. Places where you can do something really different, really adventurous.

How about taking an airplane ride where you don't sit inside the airplane, you sit out front on the wing of the aircraft?

There is this attraction near Dayton, where you can duplicate what it must have been like more than 100 years ago when humankind first learned to fly.

The first practical airplane sold to the public was developed by the Wright brothers. It was called the **Wright Model B Flyer**, and there was no cockpit.

The pilot and one passenger sat on the forward part of the lower wing. It didn't go very fast, about 50 miles per hour, but it flew.

In fact, the "Model B" was the first aircraft to carry merchandise.

It happened in 1910. A Columbus, Ohio, businessman wanted to take advantage of the news media attention being given the new fad of flying, so he contacted the Wright Brothers and asked if they could fly some fabric to his store in Columbus all the way from Dayton.

The young pilot hired for the job, Phillip Parmalee, had just been taught to fly by the Wright Brothers, and he knew nothing about the landscape between Dayton and Columbus. So Orville Wright found a road map and managed to tack it down on the wing where Parmalee could see it and figure out, by taking quick glances at the map, whether he was going in the right direction.

There were no problems. Shortly before noon on November 7, fire sirens, bells, and whistles started going off all over Columbus as the plane was spotted in the east, heading for the city. Thousands of people rushed into the streets and onto rooftops to see this airplane making history.

More than 3,000 people paid a dollar each to be in the grandstand to watch Parmalee's arrival. It was just seconds before noon when he circled the crowd one last time, then gently brought his plane in for a perfect landing in the center of a racetrack.

"It was a dandy trip," Parmalee was quoted as saying.

The modern version of the original Wright "model B" that still lets you take a ride while sitting on the wing of the aircraft.

It was more than "dandy"; it was the world's first air freight shipment, and it happened in Ohio. (For the full story of this history-making flight, see my book, *Strange Tales From Ohio*).

For a modest fee, you can get a taste of what that early pilot felt flying, become an honorary aviator, and ride a replica of the original Wright Model B Flyer, duplicating early flights by the Wrights. The replica is similar to the original in every way possible, but has some modifications to meet present-day Federal Aviation Administration safety requirements.

It all takes place in Miamisburg, south of Dayton.

The Model B Flyer is located in a building that replicates the original Wright Brothers' hangar at Huffman Prairie (now surrounded by Wright-Patterson Air Force Base) where the Wrights perfected their flying machine and taught themselves to fly.

You can see the flyable model as well as an exact replica of the one the Wright Brothers built. (One of the original Model B planes is also on display at the National Museum of the United States Air Force in Fairborn, Ohio.)

The Dayton-Wright Brothers Airport is a general aviation field, and you will find the replica of the Wrights' original hangar tucked away near the flight line.

Admission to the hangar is free. Inside, you can see both the flyable look-a-like Model B as well as an exact replica and a new, more

The Hamburger Wagon in Miamisburg, in business since 1913. Don't bother asking for ketchup.

modern, flyable version that is being constructed by a group of volunteers to supplement their original aircraft.

The pilot gave me a bit of advice as he was strapping me into my seat on the edge of the wing: "Keep your goggles on and your mouth closed in case we run into a swarm of bugs on takeoff." Talk about the wind in your face.

Two big propellers are behind you, powered by a large chain driven by a single motor. As you roar down the runway and timidly take off, you get a true bird's-eye view of flying.

Over the thunder of the motor, I shouted to the pilot a question about what was it like to fly a plane based on the earliest form of aviation. "It's kind of like driving an old tractor across a freshly plowed field," he responded. "If I want to make a turn, I have to crank the wheel 15 to 20 seconds before the turn."

The ride doesn't last very long, but in those few minutes, you join a select group of people who have gone aloft in mankind's earliest type of aircraft and you experience history flying higher and farther than Orville Wright did on his first flight at Kitty Hawk, North Carolina.

The hangar is open to the public every Tuesday, Thursday, and Saturday from 9:00 a.m. until 2:30 p.m. Orientation flights are by appointment, are usually flown on Saturdays, and are subject to the weather and the availability of pilots. In other words, call first.

There is another historic tradition in Miamisburg: lunch at the famous Hamburger Wagon.

It really is a small, enclosed wagon that has been around since 1913 serving hamburgers in downtown Miamisburg.

The legend is that Sherman "Cocky" Porter, one of the rescue workers from the big flood of 1913, started making hamburgers for other volunteers, using a secret family recipe. When the flood was over, many people begged him to continue making the burgers, so he bought a small concession wagon and started selling them commercially. Porter is long gone, but the hamburger and his recipe are still going strong.

The burgers, made from a closely guarded recipe, are cooked in oil in a large cast iron skillet. Nothing fancy here, just hamburgers with pickle or onion. There is an extra charge if you want additional pickles. Don't bother to ask for any other kind of condiment or cheese. They don't have it. Oh yes, they do offer salt and pepper. In recent years, the Hamburger Wagon has also added soft drinks and potato chips to the menu.

It's just a two-person operation, and customers line up around the block at noon to buy burgers by the bagful.

Wright B Flyer
Dayton-Wright Brothers Airport
10550 Springboro Pike • Miamisburg, OH   937-885-2327
www.wright-b-flyer.org

The Hamburger Wagon
12 E Central Ave • Miamisburg, OH   937-847-2442
www.hamburgerwagon.com

The Coolest Toys on Earth

Milford

I like picture-postcard small towns. Milford qualifies as one of those charming places you discover while driving on a winding road you may have never been on before.

A little history: "Old" Milford is located on U.S. Route 50 at the Little Miami River in Clermont County. The town was founded in the early 1800s because it was the first safe place, or ford, where people could cross the Little Miami River north of the Ohio River. There was a grist mill at the site, so it became known as the Mill Ford and later, Milford.

Today, it is a beautiful small town with quaint shops and restaurants, historic churches, including the first Methodist church in the Northwest Territory, and it is also home to a unique toy store, called, modestly, **The Coolest Toys On Earth**.

It was the brain-child of Elliot Werner, who bought a gasoline-powered scooter called a "Go-Ped" to help him get around his college campus after he managed to drop a manhole cover on his foot. The Go-Ped was such a hit that other students wanted to buy them, and a business was born.

Werner secured a small store, only 800 square feet, at 314 Main Street in Milford and crammed every wondrous, exciting, novel toy that caught his eye into the small space.

There are toys that fly, such as stomp-powered rockets, radio-controlled quadcopters, jumping bugs, and sky lanterns.

There are toys with wheels, everything from pint-size earth-moving equipment to Go-Peds, to luggage on a scooter.

There are toys that make noise, such as "Airzookas," a device that looks like a bazooka but uses safe compressed air to make a bang, and rockets that use newspaper as fuel.

There are classic wind-up toys and some that can only be described as having cutting-edge toy technology.

That's the point. Every toy in the store has to first pass Elliot's personal inspection before it can be put on the shelf for sale. He personally plays with it, and unless he gets excited about the item and exclaims that "it's the coolest toy on earth," the toy does not get space in his store.

In warm weather, many of his discoveries spill out on the sidewalk in front of the store.

When we took a One Tank Trip to visit Elliot back in 2013, he was out in front of the store playing with an air-powered, foam-tipped bow and arrow that would send an arrow almost the length of a city-block toward a target. He also demonstrated a sort-of pocket go-kart that went roaring up a steep hillside street. It was obvious that Elliot takes childlike delight in every toy he sells.

This is one toy store that will appeal to all the kids in the family, including the adults who still have a bit of the child in them.

Coolest Toys on Earth
314 Main St • Milford, OH   513-831-8697
www.coolesttoysonearth.com

For more ideas in the area, see other chapters in this book or:

Clermont County Convention and Visitors Bureau
www.visitclermontohio.com • 513-732-3600

Petting the Lake Erie Sea Monster

Urbana

Would you like to pet the creature many scientists believe might be the legendary Lake Erie sea monster?

For many years, marine biologists have suggested that the monster reported to have been seen in Lake Erie is probably a fish. A really big fish. Probably a sturgeon.

Sturgeon have been known to grow to more than 20 feet in length and weigh more than 1,500 pounds.

In fact, they were almost fished to extinction in the Great Lakes in the early 1900s. Sturgeon were much in demand at one time for their eggs, which are more commonly known as caviar. At one time, Sandusky was known as the "Caviar Capital of the World."

There is a place in central Ohio where you can actually pet a sturgeon.

Freshwater Farms of Ohio, located in Urbana, has a Sturgeon Petting Zoo.

It is actually a farm that raises fish and other aquatic creatures as its main crop.

The sturgeon, about four feet long, can be found in an aquatic zoo in the main barn, which houses the hatchery for the farm.

Admission is free, and the young sturgeon, swimming around in what appears to be a huge toddler's swimming pool, seem to enjoy the attention and fondling.

Despite their size and the fact that their tail resembles a shark's, sturgeon have no teeth. They use their mouth like a vacuum cleaner to collect the smaller aquatic creatures they feed on.

The farm also raises rainbow trout, and you can feed the trout, which seem to always be hungry. There are dispensers near the trout tanks, and for a quarter, you get a handful of food pellets that the fish just love. Toss a few into the tank, and the water suddenly roils as thousands of trout scramble for the food.

Elsewhere in the hatchery, you will find other sea life on exhibit, such as frogs, salamanders, shrimp, and even an alligator named Fluffy.

A youngster shows his excitement, petting a four-foot long sturgeon. *(Freshwater Farms)*

The farm sells fish for stocking ponds as well as plants for water gardens. They even have koi and goldfish.

A store at the farm also sells fresh prepared trout. You can get fresh, smoked, or frozen trout fillets to take home, as well as a host of related products.

The petting zoo and retail store are open year-round during regular business hours.

While you are in the neighborhood, just down the road is another attraction that I like.

The **Champaign Aviation Museum** is located at nearby Grimes Field Airport in Urbana.

This is home to an under-construction World War II B-17 bomber nicknamed "The Champaign Lady."

Volunteers have been working on the giant plane for 10 years, and the hope is, when it is completed, it will once again take to the skies and be permanently based at the museum.

In the meantime, you can see up close the work going on and even talk with some of the volunteers who are rebuilding the aircraft.

The museum also has on display a flying B-25 bomber from World War II as well as a C-47, which was the freight-hauling workhorse of that war, and many other smaller aircraft that are equally historic.

Unlike many museums that have their exhibits roped off, you can actually climb into some of these aircraft to get an up-close look at the controls and the facilities that GIs had to use during the war.

Another thing that sets this museum apart is the fact they do not charge admission.

By the way, while you are at the airport, be sure to stop in at the **Airport Cafe** and try the pie. They make many different kinds of pie each day, and some people fly in from great distances just for a piece of fresh, homemade pie.

Freshwater Farms of Ohio
2624 US Hwy 68 • Urbana, OH   937-652-3701
www.fwfarms.com

Champaign Aviation Museum
Grimes Field
1652 N Main St • Urbana, OH   937-652-4710
www.champaignaviationmuseum.org

Airport Cafe
Grimes Field
1636 N Main St • Urbana, OH   937-652-2010
www.airportcafeurbana.com

For more ideas in the area, see other chapters in this book or:

Champaign County Convention and Visitor's Bureau
www.champaignoh.com • 217-351-4133

Another Way to Enjoy the Water

Fairfield

For thousands of years, ever since the Polynesians spotted a piece of floating timber in the ocean and climbed aboard to ride the waves to shore, humans have been finding new ways to enjoy riding on water.

In 1922, 18-year-old Ralph Samuelson of Minnesota decided that if he could ski on snow, he could also ski on water, and a new water sport was born.

The problem with water skiing and many other wakeboard types of equipment is that they have to be towed by a boat or there have to be big, rolling waves. But now, there is a unique attraction in southwestern Ohio that lets you enjoy the thrill of speeding across the water without being pulled by a watercraft.

Wake Nation is one of only a handful of cable wake parks in the United States, and the only one presently in Ohio.

The park has a 10-acre oval lake with cables running overhead that tow as many as six people at a time at speeds from 18 to 20 mph around the lake.

Wakeboarding, by the way, is a combination of water skiing and snowboarding, but the board used here is slightly larger than a snowboard. A spokesman for Wake Nation, Bill Mefford, said that the lake is set up so everyone, from beginners to experienced wakeboarders, will enjoy their ride. "The beginners usually stay on their knees until they get accustomed to the ride and learn how the cable works," he explained.

Unfortunately, I am a bit old to be standing on a fast-moving wakeboard, so I asked my son-in-law Peter Luttmann and my grandson Ryan Luttmann, who was in his teens, to try it in my place.

Ryan said, "When you're looking at the people from shore, it doesn't look like it's going very fast, but when you are on the cable, on the water, it's very fast!"

His father, an experienced snow skier, agreed, adding it is not as easy as it looks, and it took him several attempts to be able to stand up on the wakeboard.

Ride a wake board without a boat at Wake Nation. Riders can reach speeds of 18 mph. towed by overhead cables that run around the 20-plus-acre lake.

This one-of-a-kind attraction has been around now for several years and attracts large crowds of young adults and families who enjoy skiing and watersports.

Ryan Luttmann said, "By my second ride, I was able to make it three times around the course. It was awesome!"

It takes about a minute, if everything goes right, to circle the lake. If you fall off your board, the cable keeps on going and a new rider hooks up. The fallen rider swims to shore (the manmade lake is about eight feet deep.) and walks back to the pier to stand in line and wait for his or her turn to get back on the cable. At the pier, there are three ways to launch a rider. The easiest is to sit on a bench and wait for the cable to come overhead and pull you onto the lake. Another way involves standing on a ramp and waiting for the cable to snag you into the lake. The third, and most difficult launch, is to stand on a bench and jump into the water just as the cable catches your line. Most folks, especially first-timers, use the sitting position to get started.

An experienced wakeboarder, Adam "A.C." Clark of Cincinnati, who told me he spends three to four days a week at the park after work, says the best part about cable versus being towed by a boat is that up to six people can get on the cables at the same time. "There is nothing better than watching your friends rippin' it up while you're riding right behind them," he said.

A.C. also pointed out that, unless you own a boat, Wake Nation is a far less expensive way to enjoy wakeboarding. It allows someone who doesn't want to buy or rent a boat and all the expensive equipment to participate in the sport at this special location.

The park also offers ramps and jumps for the more experienced wakeboarders.

It is a great One Tank Trip, and a new way to enjoy the water in the summertime.

Wake Nation
201 Joe Nuxhall Way • Fairfield, OH   513-887-WAKE
www.wakenation.com

Fairfield is a suburb of Cincinnati, and offers many things to do and places to stay. For more ideas, see:

Butler County Visitors Bureau
www.gettothebc.com • 513-860-4194

Really Big Electric Train Layout

West Chester

We all know someone who loves trains. Well, here's a place for anyone who has ever had an electric train or a fascination with railroading. It is billed as the "Largest Indoor Train Display in the World," and after you spend a couple of hours walking around its thousands of feet of track, you will agree that the claim is no exaggeration.

EnterTRAINment Junction is the brainchild of Don Oeters, a model train hobbyist, who, after a successful business career, has turned his energies toward creating a train-themed tourist destination in a Cincinnati suburb.

What was once a huge furniture warehouse has been converted into a Disney-esque structure that features several train-related attractions under one roof.

As you enter the building, you find yourself in a replica of a small-town American village of the 1890s. Old-fashioned street lights line a cobblestone street that leads to a train station. The street is lined by stores that offer train-related hobby materials and food, all disguised with façades from another era.

The main attraction is the exhibition hall where the massive model train display is running. The trains are all G-gauge, sometimes known as "garden trains." Each car is about the size of a loaf of bread, and the scenery, buildings, cars, trees, and people are all modeled on the same scale.

The display covers 25,000 square feet, which means it's nearly half the size of a football field.

There are winding aisles that wander back and forth across the display, tracing the nearly two miles of tiny railroad tracks that wend their way through manmade mountains and tunnels, past rivers and lakes, and alongside a towering 11-foot waterfall. At any given time, more than 1,200 railroad cars, making up some 90 trains, are running, circling the display, crossing bridges and trestles, passing through tunnels, and whistling through small villages. The trains can be seen mostly at a waist-high level, but they also climb to 11 feet above the walkway in some of the mountain exhibits.

EnterTRAINment Junction bills itself as "the largest indoor train display in the world."

The exhibition area has wide walkways with lots of benches, drinking fountains, and clean restrooms. A large amount of Plexiglas is used to protect the trains and scenery from inquisitive hands, but it also takes away from the realism of the displays and makes taking photographs of the collection difficult. My hope is that they remove some of the Plexiglas on the second-level observation area to allow visitors, especially those with cameras, a clear bird's-eye view of the entire layout.

The attention to detail in the models is incredible, thanks to more than 100 volunteer model train enthusiasts who contributed their model-making skills to bring this display to life, creating the scenery and vistas that include real water-filled river rapids, tiny coal mining towns clinging to the sides of mountains, big-city streets, and factories, all scaled to size. For example, there is a car show in one area, complete with classic model cars with their hoods open and even tiny trophies for the best cars.

Don Oeters told me that the entire train room is a work in progress and that hundreds of new details and additions are planned, such as a working canal lock, an incline railroad, and a hot air balloon that will take off and fly from one scene to another, all faithfully copied in same scale as the trains. "Every time you visit EnterTRAINment Junction, there will be something new to see," he said.

One of the latest attractions is a G-gauge replica of Cincinnati's iconic amusement park, Coney Island. Located on the mezzanine area, the miniature rides all work, and there is even music playing in the tiny dance hall. In front of the park, models of the trolleys that used to bring customers to the park stop and go.

Using historically accurate buildings and scenery, along with model trains of the period, the model also helps teach history. Three distinct railroad eras are represented, starting with the 1830s to the 1890s, the era of steam locomotives. Then it moves on to the middle period of the 1900s to 1950s, when diesel locomotives came on the scene. Finally, the model turns to the period from 1960 to today.

Besides the model train exhibit, there is an area off the main street that holds an old-fashioned amusement park funhouse, where you walk through a rolling barrel and rooms where optical illusions abound. There is a hall of mirrors that creates a maze. At Christmas-time, this area is turned into a holiday fantasy land that incorporates the fun-house attractions.

On another side of the train exhibit is a train-themed playroom, Imagination Junction, for youngsters. There are lots of things for the kids to do and a place where they can run, climb, crawl, and burn off some energy.

EnterTRAINment Junction
7379 Squire Ct • West Chester, OH   513-898-8000
www.entertrainmentjunction.com

The West Chester and Cincinnati areas offer a lot of things to do. Check other chapters in this book for some ideas, or contact:

Butler County Visitors Bureau
www.gettothebc.com • 513-860-4194

SOUTHEAST OHIO

Discover The Hocking Hills

Logan, Rockbridge, South Bloomingville

One of my truly favorite places in Ohio is the Hocking Hills, southeast of Columbus.

In the winter there are frozen waterfalls, stark canyons with cliff walls decorated with fringes of icicles, snow-covered woods broken by stands of ancient evergreens, scenic caves and icy lakes. You will find cozy cabins and inns with roaring fireplaces and hot tubs where, on dark nights, you can clearly see the dome of stars overhead.

There are so many natural attractions in this area for every season of the year that it is often hard to pick just a few that I consider "must-see" attractions.

To start, I would say that **Ash Cave** is in this category. In fact, even with my claustrophobia, I don't mind going inside this cave.

It is one of the most accessible caves in the region, but it really isn't a cave, just a huge outcropping of rock that forms an almost cathedral-like natural amphitheater at the base of a small waterfall.

To get to the cave, you have to leave your car in a parking lot along State Route 56. Signs guide you on the quarter-mile trail that leads from the parking lot to the cave. It will take about a half-an-hour to walk the distance, which, incidentally, is wheelchair accessible.

The trail is surrounded by giant hemlock trees. As you get closer to the cave wall, you hear the whisper and splash of falling waters.

The Hocking Hills offers a thrilling zip line course that takes riders above the trees and across the Hocking River.

The early settlers named the cave for the huge piles of ash that were found at the entrance to the cave. There are several explanations for the ashes. Most believe that they were left by the many tribes of Native Americans who, at one time or another, camped in the cave. Others claim early settlers and Native Americans used the area to smelt lead and silver from the nearby rocks. Whatever, the modern-day discoverers of the cave found a pile of ashes 100 feet long by 30 feet wide and three to four feet deep.

The waterfall comes tumbling more than 100 feet from a small tributary of the East Fork of Queer Creek. It forms a small pool at the mouth of the cave. Every season of the year the amount of water changes and makes a visit anytime unforgettable.

The best-known attraction in the Hocking Hills is perhaps **Old Man's Cave**, which got its name from an old hermit, Richard Rowe, who lived in the cave in the late 1700s.

Today, the cave, located on State Route 664 at the upper falls, is the start of the Grandma Gatewood Trail that stretches through the hills for six miles connecting three of the park areas. "Grandma" Gatewood was Emma Gatewood, the first woman to hike the entire 2,168 miles of the Appalachian Trail.

If hiking is too tame for you and your family, then **Hocking Hills Canopy Tours** is another way to get a high-up view of the forests and valleys of the area.

Hocking Hills Canopy Tours was the first professional zip line business in the state of Ohio. The line takes you on a treetop tour of acres of forest floors, caves, rock cliffs, and even crosses over the Hocking River. In addition to the zip lines are some spectacular rope bridges that add extra excitement to the course.

Give yourself plenty of time. It usually takes two to three hours to complete the entire zip line course.

You have to be at least age 10 to participate and weigh less than 250 pounds.

Another scenic way to see the Hocking Hills is by boat.

The **Hocking Hills Canoe Livery** has been around since 1995, and offers rental canoes, kayaks, and inflatable rafts.

They offer a series of different trips, the most popular being a two- to three- hour ride on the Hocking River, where you pass small islands, sandbars, and get a different view of the hills and caves that have made this one of the top tourist destinations in Ohio. In fact, at one point, you will be able to see the zip liners as they fly through the trees high above the river.

Ash Cave
27291 State Rte 56 • South Bloomingville, OH

Old Man's Cave
Hocking Hills State Park Visitors Center
State Rte 664 • Logan, OH   740-385-8003

Hocking Hills Canopy Tour
10714 Jackson St • Rockbridge, OH   740-385-9477
www.hockinghillscanopytours.com

Hocking Hills Canoe Livery
12789 State Rte 664 S • Logan, OH   740-385-0523
www.hockingriver.com

There are nine state parks and countless other things to do in the Hocking Hills. For more ideas, visit:

Hocking Hills Regional Welcome Center
13178 State Rte 664 Scenic • Logan, OH   740-385-9706
www.hockinghills.com

A Memorial to Ohio Giants

McConnelsville

It was a stormy late-summer night on September 3, 1925. High in the sky over Noble County in southeastern Ohio was the pride of the U.S. Navy, the USS *Shenandoah*. The world's first rigid airship, filled with helium gas, was fighting for its very life.

The *Shenandoah* was 680 feet long, the distance of two football fields laid end-to-end. She had a poetic name that means "daughter of the stars." *Shenandoah* carried a crew of 43, weighed 38 tons, and had a range of 5,000 miles—an incredible distance for its time.

However, it was no match for the violent thunderstorm it encountered over southeastern Ohio. A sudden updraft caught the ship and carried it higher than the pressure limits of its helium gas bags. They burst, tearing the ship into three pieces. Fourteen of the crew, including the commanding officer, Cdr. Zachary Lansdowne from Greenville, were killed when the section containing the main control car tore loose and fell to earth.

Amazingly, 29 crew members survived by riding three partially gas-filled sections of the aircraft to the ground.

In the 1930s, the federal government erected a memorial in downtown Ava that tells the story of the ship and lists the names of those who lost their lives in the crash. If you've traveled South on Interstate 77, just south of the I-70 intersection near Cambridge, you will see on the west side of the highway a large circle of rocks and a lone flagpole flying an American flag. It's an unofficial memorial to the ship and its crew and marks where some parts of the great airship crashed.

The Raynor family of Ava owns much of the land where the pieces of the *Shenandoah* came to earth. When Bryan Raynor was a boy, he used to follow his grandfather as he guided curious tourists to the various crash sites. Over the years, Bryan and his wife Theresa have collected many items connected with the *Shenandoah*, so many that they finally decided to build a museum to house their collection.

But the **USS Shenandoah Airship Museum** is unlike most museums. It is located in a former camper-trailer and houses the collection in glass display cases. The Raynors annually have taken their museum to schools in Noble County, as well as nursing homes, fairs, and festivals.

Many of the items are one-of-a-kind, such as a wash basin found in the wreckage, and a sugar bowl with sugar still inside. There is a huge collection of photographs, including many taken at the time of the crash.

Bryan Raynor died in 2013, but his family continues to show their trailer-museum by appointment.

Today, you will see a state historic marker in a rest stop along I-77 and I-70. It tells some of the story, but to learn far more, take a One Tank Trip to Theresa Raynor's museum on wheels.

Another giant literally shook the earth in this part of Ohio. Called Big Muskie, and considered by some to be "one of the seven engineering models of the world," it was the world's largest dragline and dug coal out of surface mines in southeastern Ohio during the late twentieth century. It was used for 22 years, and was finally taken out of service in 1991.

All that remains of the behemoth is the bucket, which is huge. The bucket alone weighs 460,000 pounds empty. It could take one bite of the earth, and that chunk could weigh 640,000 pounds. The capacity of the bucket could hold a 12-car garage. The bucket stands today as a memorial to the miners who dug Ohio coal. **Miners' Memorial Park**, with the bucket from the Big Muskie, is located along State Route 78 near the town of McConnelsville.

USS Shenandoah Airship Trailer Museum
Ava, OH   740-732-2624 (by appointment only; call first)

Miners' Memorial Park
Ohio Rte 78 (follow the signs) • McConnelsville

Big Muskie's bucket at Coal Miners' Memorial Park.

Home on the Range, Ohio-Style

Barnesville, Belmont, St. Clairsville

Imagine driving on a gravel road in southeastern Ohio, when suddenly you see a cloud of dust ahead and hear the bawling of cattle. Lots of cattle. All at once, over a slight rise in the road came a herd of wild-eyed, long-horned steers. You are actually in the middle of a real, honest-to-gosh cattle drive.

No, you're not in Texas. You are in Belmont County, home to the largest registered Texas longhorn cattle ranch east of San Francisco, California.

How did a huge herd of Texas longhorn cattle end up in Ohio? Darol Dickinson, one of the owners, told me the ranch started out in Colorado, but after a particularly bad year with snowstorms, drought and high feed bills, he spotted some reclaimed strip mine land in Belmont County where the grass grew so high in the summer that it could "reach the belly of a steer." He and his family decided to become Buckeyes and moved their ranch to Barnesville.

Located along Interstate Route 70, the **Dickinson Cattle Company** ranch is open for tours from June until Labor Day. They even have old school buses painted to look like cowhides that they use to transport visitors around the sprawling ranch.

The tours started, says Dickinson, when they first began ranching in Ohio. Curious people going by would spot the longhorn steers and stop in to see what was going on.

"We couldn't get anything done," says Dickinson. The choice was to either be unfriendly and post "no trespassing" signs or open the ranch to visitors.

They bought the old school buses and hired someone to give the tours. Today, they are a major tourist attraction in Belmont County.

They don't just raise Texas longhorns; they also have a herd of African Watusi cattle as well as an unusual Dutch breed called BueLingo.

BueLingos are easy to spot because they are all black with a big white center band around their bellies.

If you visit the ranch, don't expect to see lots of cowboys on horse-

Dickinson Cattle Company is a real longhorn steer range right here in Ohio.

back herding cattle. The cowboys here usually wear baseball caps and ride small, quick, four-wheel drive ATVs. Dickinson says they would like to use horses, but the hilly Ohio terrain makes using mechanical horses more practical.

Besides the cattle, visitors also can see some of the ranch operations and visit the ranch store, where they can buy longhorn steaks and other products.

As word of the ranch has spread, the tourism business has grown. Dickinson has added two new privies at the welcome center to the ranch. (Actually, although the buildings resemble outhouses, they are modern bathrooms with running water and all the necessary features. They are even handicapped accessible.)

Another reason to make a One Tank Trip to Belmont County is it is the only county in the state of Ohio with not one, but three official "Ohio Byways." They are Ohio Route 147 and 800, known as the "Drovers Trail"; the Ohio River Scenic Byway, Route 7; and the old National Road, U.S. Route 40. There is incredible scenery on all three routes.

Speaking of U.S. Route 40, it's home to one of my favorite lunchtime restaurants in Ohio, **Mehlman's Cafeteria** in St. Clairsville. It's an old-fashioned-style cafeteria where a platoon of workers stand behind the counter and fill your plate with any of hundreds of choices as you move down the serving line. Everything, from the breads to the pies, is made from scratch in the kitchen each morning. The prices are very reasonable, service is fast, and the food tastes good. Specialties include baked steak, broccoli casserole, and apple dumplings with homemade ice cream.

Every day, you'll find people from three states eating here.

If you are into nostalgia, this is where the last Mail Pouch barn painter once lived. The late Harley Warrick, of Belmont, was the last of a number of painters who traveled throughout the Midwest, painting Mail Pouch Tobacco signs on barns. You can see one of the barns that Harley painted at **Barkcamp State Park**.

The park offers more than 1,200 acres of rolling woods and hills. There is year-round camping, picnic areas, and some good fishing in the lake inside the park. There is also a special handicapped access area.

Dickinson Cattle Company
35000 Muskrat Rd • Barnesville, OH   740-758-5050
www.texaslonghorn.com

Mehlman's Cafeteria
51800 National Rd E • St Clairsville, OH   740-695-2098
www.mehlman.com

Barkcamp State Park
65330 Barkcamp Park Rd • Belmont, OH   740-484-4064
www.ohiodnr.com

Adventures on a Riverboat

Marietta

One of the really unforgettable people I met early in my career of traveling Ohio was Capt. James Sands of Marietta, owner and skipper of the **Valley Gem**, an authentic sternwheeler that carries tourists on the Muskingum and Ohio Rivers.

The *Valley Gem* has been, and continues to be, a symbol of Marietta and all the great riverboats that have called at this oldest city in the Northwest Territory. Thousands of tourists have been introduced to the romance of the sternwheel riverboat by Jim Sands, his family, and his crew, and dozens have been proposed to and married on board the *Valley Gem*.

The slow riverboat is the perfect way to see the confluence of the Muskingum and Ohio Rivers, to sometimes see deer swimming across the Ohio, wave to passing river boats pushing a string of barges as big as a football field. On trips up the Muskingum, the *Valley Gem* often goes through the historic hand-operated locks on the river as boats have done for nearly two centuries.

Captain Sands was always a favorite with kids, especially when he would invite them into the pilot house and offer to let them take the wheel of the ship as it pounded away upriver.

Jim Sands' brother, Air Force Maj. Gen. Harry Sands, once commanded much of the Intercontinental Ballistic Missile program.

My photographer that day, Bill West, and I were shooting a story about the *Valley Gem*. Major General Sands was visiting. He volunteered to captain a small motor boat to take photographer West around the much larger *Valley Gem* as we proceeded up the Muskingum River.

It had recently rained, and the river was muddy and full of tree limbs. While West was shooting video of the sternwheeler, Major General Sands, who was driving the little boat, apparently was watching what West was doing and not paying too much attention to where he was driving his small, speedy motorboat. He hit a large limb and the impact lifted the smaller boat right out of the water. Photographer West nearly ended upside-down in the surprised man's lap.

The *Valley Gem* sternwheeler on the Ohio River.

I was standing on the bridge of the *Valley Gem* with Capt. Jim Sands. We had watched the smaller boat suddenly leap out of the water, and over the splashing sound of the giant paddlewheel on our boat, we could hear West yelling obscenities at the general. Capt. Sands smiled and said, "I don't think the general has ever been told off quite like that before."

Both men, and the video, survived the incident.

My friend Jim Sands passed away in 1998 after a quarter of a century as a riverboat captain. His son Jason has taken over the reins, and today, Capt. Jason Sands and his lifelong friend Capt. Don Sandford continue touring two great rivers with a new, larger *Valley Gem*.

It still is one of the best ways to see the Ohio River and get a taste of what travel in America was like almost 200 years ago.

Valley Gem Sternwheeler
601 Front St • Marietta, OH   740-373-7862
www.valleygemsternwheeler.com

For more ideas in the area, contact:

Marietta-Washington County Convention & Visitors Bureau
www.mariettaohio.org • 740-373-5178

A Park with a View

Clarington, Fly

I've said it before and I'll say it again: Ohio's jewels are its Metropark and county park systems.

So many wonderful examples spring to mind: the Cleveland Metroparks with their access to Lake Erie and the rivers that feed the lake. The step back into history at Slate Run Farm, just one of the many great parks in the Columbus area. The covered bridges cared for lovingly in the Ashtabula County Metroparks. When you are looking for something to do, always remember to check your local and county parks first.

One of my favorite parks in the entire state is a very small one that offers only some picnic tables and hiking trails. It is located in one of Ohio's most sparsely populated counties.

I am referring to **Kiedaisch Point Park** in Monroe County in southeastern Ohio, overlooking the Ohio River.

Bear in mind that the population of Monroe County at the time of this writing is fewer than 15,000 people. They live in some of Ohio's most rugged terrain, which the county proudly proclaims to be "Ohio's Switzerland."

You might think you are in the Alps when you climb the 500 feet to Kiedaisch Point Park. On a clear day, you can see seven miles of the Ohio River Valley unrolling in every direction.

As I said, there is not a lot to do, but so much here to entertain the eye and satisfy the soul. Bring along a picnic lunch and your camera and enjoy the hiking paths that lead up to the top of the point where you will find some picnic tables.

Monroe County is also home to a very small community with the unusual name of Fly. Fly reportedly got its name when a community meeting was being held to come up with a new name because the U.S. Post Office did not like "Stringtown," the name the community had been using. As town fathers gathered to pick a new name, a fly landed on the nose of one of the community members. The man suggested, "Why don't we call it 'Fly'?" and the idea was approved.

Fly is just across the Ohio River from Sistersville, West Virginia. The

The Sistersville Ferry connects Ohio and West Virginia. *(Marietta-Washington County CVB)*

two states are linked by the historic **Sistersville Ferry** boat that chugs across the river whenever a car or truck pulls up to the edge of the river and flashes its headlights or blows its horn. It is one of the very few ferry boats still operating on the river.

The boat, based in West Virginia, has been plagued with financial problems the last few years, and currently only operates Thursday through Sunday. If you want to ride the ferry, rather than drive a dozen miles to the nearest bridge, it would be a good idea to call first to make sure it's running.

If you are looking for a scenic getaway or a glimpse of what Ohio may have been 100 years ago, this is a perfect lazy One Tank Trip.

Kiedaisch Point Park
Monroe County Parks
52100-52698 Township Rd 419 • Clarington, OH   740-472-1341

The Sistersville Ferry
Fly, OH   304-771-8398

For more ideas in the area, contact:

Marietta–Washington County Convention & Visitors Bureau
www.mariettaohio.org • 740-373-5178

Zanesville, a Monumental City

Zanesville

Zanesville has always been one of my favorite towns for a One Tank Trip. It was Ohio's second state capital. Its Victorian wedding-cake courthouse serves as county seat for Muskingum County. It has a working sternwheel riverboat, and the downtown is dotted with unique sculptures. Those are just a few of the attractions that led me to this central Ohio gem.

Let's start with the claim to being the second capital of Ohio. The Ohio legislature did, indeed, move the original capital from Chillicothe to Zanesville in 1810 because powerful politicians at the time would only lend their support to certain legislation if the capital was moved to Zanesville. The legislation passed, and the state capital became Zanesville. In fact, three local bigwigs built the Stone Academy Building in the Putnam District to be used as the new capitol building. The Stone Academy Building still stands, but after moving to Zanesville in 1810, the state legislature moved the capital back to Chillicothe in 1812. But in 1816, the peripatetic legislature again moved the state capital, this time to Columbus, where it has been ever since.

As for the courthouse, it was built in 1874, and is perhaps one of the most beautiful county courthouses in the entire state. In recent years, the exterior has been restored to give it much the same appearance as it had in the 1800s.

The **Lorena**, a true sternwheel boat, has a rich history. Named for a similar ship that once carried freight and passengers on the Muskingum, the name comes from the song, "Lorena," about lost love that was inspired by a romance between a man and woman from Zanesville. The song was very popular with Civil War soldiers.

The modern-day *Lorena* was purchased by the Chamber of Commerce in 1976 in the hope of attracting tourists to Zanesville. It has done that job for more than 40 years.

But my favorite attraction in Zanesville is the eclectic artwork scattered along South 6th Street and on top of a building at 110 South 6th Street. Here, high on a rooftop overlooking downtown Zanesville, you will see the larger-than-life sculpted figure of famed Native American

Iroquois Chief Nemacolin with his arms outstretched to the clouds above. Along the street, you find statues of horses, working men, and miscellaneous other works of art, all from the talented hands of sculptor **Alan Cottrill**. Cottrill, a Zanesville native, moved his studios and gallery to his hometown from Washington, Pennsylvania, in 2003.

Zanesville is also one of Ohio's pottery centers, and you can tour some of the factories, such as Hartstone Pottery, and visit company stores, where you can find some bargains and hard-to-find pieces.

If you like travel history, remember that Zanesville is also home to the famous "Y" bridge. It's an actual bridge that spans the confluence of the Muskingum and Licking Rivers. Local folks love to given directions to Linden Avenue by telling strangers, "Just drive to the middle of the bridge and turn left."

Lorena Sternwheeler
Docked at Zane's Landing Park • Zanesville, OH   800-743-2303
www.visitzanesville.info/lorena-sternwheeler

Alan Cottrill Sculpture Studio and Gallery
110 S 6th St • Zanesville, OH   740-453-9822
www.alancottrill.com

For more ideas in the area, see other chapters in this book or:

Visit Zanesville
www.visitzanesville.info • 800-743-2303

The beautiful Muskingum County Courthouse in Zanesville.

OUTSIDE OHIO

Beef-on-Weck, Sponge Candy, and a Boat Ride Through a Cave

New York: Lockport, Silver Creek, Williamsville

Every time I take a trip to the Buffalo, New York, area, I think of three things: beef-on-weck, sponge candy, and a boat ride through a cave alongside the Erie Canal.

In western New York, there is this unique attraction: a manmade cave on a hillside above the famed Erie Canal that offers a boat ride down a stream inside the cave.

To begin, **Lockport Cave** was the product of the digging of the Erie Canal in the early 1800s. Some businessmen in Lockport realized they could put the surplus water from the canal to good use. By digging a quarter-mile tunnel on a hillside overlooking the canal, they could pump water into it and, using gravity, create water power for the mills and businesses above. The big problem was, the hillside was solid dolomite, a hard rock. It took workers in the mid-1800s nearly eight years to carve out a quarter-mile-long tunnel, but it was a success. The tunnel's water power was used until 1941.

The tunnel sat empty for many years until it was purchased in the 1970s by a local entrepreneur, Tom Callahan, who first recognized the possibility of turning the tunnel into a tourist attraction.

Carved out of stone, the tunnel is always about 55 degrees Fahrenheit. Water seeps through the stone above in places, and geological formations on the stone give it a spooky, cavelike appearance. There is a small stream that has been naturally created by the leaking water near the end of the cave. Because the water gets no sunlight, it contains no living organisms and is only about two feet deep. A flat bottom boat with an electric motor takes visitors for a silent ride down the stream. With the dim electric lights, the dripping overhead water, and the silent glide through the darkness, all I could think of was the scene from the play, *The Phantom of the Opera*, in which the Phantom glides through the catacombs of Paris.

The boat ride is said to be the longest cave boat ride in the United States. It is about 800 feet long.

When you finally exit the cave, you find yourself actually looking down on some of the locks of the Erie Canal.

Unlike Ohio, where only bits and pieces of the old canal are still in existence, in New York, the canal still works and is used mostly for recreation.

The tour of the tunnel and the boat ride can take about 70 minutes. Wear comfortable shoes for walking and bring along a light sweater or jacket.

Lockport is next door to Buffalo, which is home to a western New York delicacy that some chain restaurants have tried to duplicate on a national scale but nothing tops the original beef-on-weck served by Charlie Roesch, owner of **Charlie the Butcher's Kitchen**.

For the uninitiated, beef-on-weck is thinly-sliced pieces of steam-ship round roast beef that has been slowly cooked for hours. The beef is piled on a kimmelweck roll that is coated on top with corn starch and a liberal amount of sea salt. A bit of *jus* is poured over the beef, and a dollop of fresh horseradish is added. One sandwich is never enough.

Charlie Roesch is the king of beef-on-weck, as far as I am concerned. Since our first meeting in the early 1990s, I have made countless trips to his single-story restaurant in Williamsville, New York, just one mile from the Buffalo airport.

I love odd things, so when I spotted a store that sold both home-made candy and concrete lawn decorations on our trip to the Buffalo area, I was hooked.

Valvo's Candies and concrete business has been a fixture in the tiny western New York town of Silver Creek for three generations.

They sell hundreds of different kinds of hand-made chocolates, but what they are known for is another western New York specialty,

Valvo's Candies sells candy, of course—and concrete lawn decorations. *(Valvo's Candies)*

sponge candy. Sponge candy is only made during autumn, after the heat of summer has passed. It is a delicate, sugary, honeycomb-like center covered with chocolate that literally melts in your mouth.

Joe Valvo, the candy maker, told me that every September, when the first batch of the year is made, they usually have a line of customers in front of the store waiting for the candy.

Now, about the concrete side of things. The parking lot and front of the store are lined with concrete bird baths, lawn statuary, and stone angels. It all started some years ago when one of the Valvo family, probably looking at the wall in the store decorated with old candy molds, thought that candy isn't the only thing you can make in a mold, and decided to make some concrete lawn ornaments to bring in some extra cash in the spring and summer. It worked.

Lockport Cave & Underground Boat Ride
5 Gooding St • Lockport, NY   716-438-0174
www.lockportcave.com

Charlie the Butcher's Kitchen
1065 Wehrle Dr • Williamsville, NY   716-633-8330
www.charliethebutcher.com

Valvo's Candies
1277 NY Rte 5 • Silver Creek, NY   716-934-2535
www.valvoscandy.com

My Most Exciting One Tank Trip

New York: Lewiston

When I am really pressed, I will admit that a trip to Ontario, Canada, or, more precisely, Niagara Falls, is my most exciting trip.

First, a little back story.

Many years ago, I met a whitewater rafting guide, John Kinney, a native of Canton, Ohio, while doing a story on whitewater rafting in Ohiopyle, Pennsylvania.

I met John again in 1992, when he opened Whirlpool Jet Boats on the Canadian side of the Niagara River in the beautiful town of Niagara-on-the-Lake.

While, for many years, the *Maid of the Mist* has been carrying tourists and sailing to the foot of Niagara Falls, commercial boating of the lower river has been infrequent because of the dangerous rapids and giant whirlpool downriver from the falls.

Commercial tours of the lower Niagara River had been halted by the U.S. and Canadian Coast Guards in the 1970s after a rafting company tragically lost three people in an accident on the river rapids when they were swept out of an inflatable boat. A fourth person, one of the rescuers, suffered a heart attack and died while attempting to save some of the victims.

It wasn't until John Kinney and his company came along with powerful jet boats and proved to the Coast Guard's satisfaction that they could safely traverse the river's 20-foot-high waves and 25 mph current that tourists were once more allowed to witness the beauty and wild energy of this famed waterway.

Over the years, I have taken the **Whirlpool Jet Boat** several times, often to do a new story on the adventure and sometimes for the sheer excitement with only my family.

One of the more memorable trips was with Fox 8 TV videographer Jim Pijor and my son, Craig.

Let me point out that Jim Pijor does not like the water. In fact, he does not know how to swim. One of our goals on that trip was to maneuver the jet boat in the rapids, close to a rounded rock with a small flat spot on top. Remember, this is one of the fastest, deepest

You're going to get wet on the Whirlpool Jet Boat. *(Whirlpool Jet Boat Rides)*

rivers in the world. Pijor, who does not lack for courage, was carrying about 70 pounds of video gear and was supposed to step off the bobbing craft and scramble up this rock to take pictures of the boat coming back downriver through the waves, some 20 feet high.

Just as Pijor was about to step off the boat onto the rock a wave lifted the craft several feet above the rock. Pijor was already in motion, and had no choice but to jump. He landed on the rock and teetered for a minute, top-heavy with the video equipment, nearly toppling into the raging emerald-green water rushing by. The sigh of relief from the crew members and me was almost audible as Jim was finally able to regain his balance and drop to his knees on the stone.

Pijor's problems didn't end there. When he was back aboard, he decided to shoot some scenes from where the captain operated the craft. The problem was, it is a very small area with just one seat at the rear of the boat. So Jim looped his arm through a metal stanchion next to the captain and, balancing the huge TV camera on his shoulder, started shooting as we entered the worst rapids on the river. Jim described it later as like being the guy carrying the football as the entire defensive line hits him. The boat hitting the waves took Pijor off his feet and slammed his shoulder repeatedly into the metal bar he was locked against, desperately hanging on. He said he was covered with bruises by the end of the day.

The tours start at the dock in Niagara-on-the-Lake. Each tourist is given a short safety lecture, and there are videos that show what the ride is like. Then you sign a release, suit up in a waterproof poncho, and line up for the boat.

The wettest part of the ride is experienced by those who grab the first couple of rows of seats, but, trust me, on this ride, everyone will get wet.

When you start upriver, the water is tranquil. The captain and crew use this time to talk about the history of this waterway separating the United States from Canada. You will be amazed at how far the water has cut back the brink of Niagara Falls. Over the years, the edge of the falls has retreated several miles.

The first excitement comes as the boat reaches the Devil's Hole Rapids. Since we are going upriver against the current, the boat has to power its way up and over the rapids. At times, it seems almost to stop dead in the rushing current before finally breaking through and once more powering up as it heads for the giant Niagara whirlpool.

From the boat you can see the famed Spanish Aerocars suspended by a thin cable, carrying tourists high above you over the valley for a bird's-eye view of the swirling waters that have claimed so many lives over the years.

The boat slows as it reaches the crook in the valley that creates the giant whirlpool. To the left stretch enormous rapids caused by the tons of water from Lake Erie that spill over the escarpment and rush down this narrow valley toward Lake Ontario. To the right, the water swirls in a huge, muddy circle before finding its way down the stone-lined canyon.

The captain warns everyone to hang on as the boat roars across the edge of the whirlpool. Minutes later, he is again shouting warnings to passengers to stow eyeglasses and cameras in waterproof bags attached to the seat in front of them.

The warnings become understandable as we approach the Devil's Hole Rapids, this time with the current.

The boat shudders as the first 10- to 15-foot waves strike the craft. Cold, green water sloshes over the passengers, especially those in the front seats.

A crew member shouts another warning to hang onto a railing attached to the back of the seat in front of them.

It is just in time because the boat suddenly dips and another wave, this one 20 feet high or more, inundates the boat. It feels as though someone has just unleashed barrels of water above your head. The water slams you into your seat. If you were foolish enough to ignore the warning about removing your glasses, they are now probably on the bottom of the river.

The waves continue to spray, splash, and pummel you as the boat plunges on through the rapids.

It is only minutes before you finally reach the calmer area below the rapids. By this time, the boat has filled almost waist deep with cold water from the river and while pumps quickly drain the boat, the craft is picking up speed. Even on a very warm day, the speed, coupled with wet clothes, can make it uncomfortably cool.

You can only imagine how wet we were on the day we filmed our story because we had to take the ride several times to get all the shots we needed for a television report.

This is a one-of-a-kind attraction.

By the way, you don't have to go to Canada to ride the Whirlpool Jet Boat. Several years ago, the operator opened a second dock on the American side of the river in Lewiston, New York, about 10 minutes from Niagara Falls. That means that you don't have to worry about passports or going through customs at the border.

Whirlpool Jet Boat Tours
61 Melville St • Niagara-on-the-Lake, Ontario, Canada
115 S Water St • Lewiston, New York, USA
www.whirlpooljet.com   888-438-4444

If you are planning to spend more than a day in Niagara Falls and surrounding areas and want more ideas, contact:

NiagaraUSA
www.Niagara-USA.com • 877-FALLS-US

Go To Hell

Go to Hell! I have wanted to tell some of my viewers, especially those who like the state of Michigan, to go to Hell for many years.

Hell, Michigan, that is.

Hell, in case you are interested, is located near Ann Arbor. By the way, Hell does freeze over. Almost every year.

OK, enough of the bad jokes. Hell is really just a wide spot in the road. Depending on who you talk to, the population is between 75 and 300. There are just a handful of businesses, including an ice cream parlor, a restaurant and convenience store, a U.S. Weather Service station; and a post office. Oh yes. There is also a very small church that seats only eight people. It's available for weddings.

Hell proclaims itself a "little town on the way up."

There are several versions of how the town was named, but the most likely one is credited to a pioneer named George Reeves who first settled in the area. When asked what he wanted to call the place, he responded, "I don't care. Call it 'Hell' if you want to."

For many years, the self-proclaimed "mayor" of Hell has been local businessman John Colone, whose unique sense of humor and background made him the right man for the job. Colone grew up in Hell, spent some time in the real hell of the Vietnam War, and was so seriously wounded in battle that he was declared dead. He had been placed in a body bag when someone noticed he was still moving. He spent 22 months in a hospital, recovering.

Colone later became a car dealer in nearby Pinckney, Michigan. In 2000, when a couple of businesses came up for sale in Hell, he decided to try to help make the town a family-friendly tourist stop using the unique town name.

For openers, he had a restaurant named Hell's Kitchen that offered pizza, sandwiches, and some daily specials. Today, it is called the Hell Hole Diner. Inside the restaurant's souvenir shop is an official U.S. Post Office for Hell. Colone says, "We do a big business sending out folks' alimony checks. We singe each letter and stamp it: 'I've been through Hell.'"

It's official: Hell sometimes freezes over.

Next door is the official U.S. Weather Service station in Hell, where they prove that many places are "hotter than Hell."

There are also Screams Ice Cream, the Hell Creek miniature golf course (the largest handicapped miniature golf course in Michigan), and the Wedding Chapel in Hell, a small, non-denominational building that seats eight and is in great demand for weddings. In fact Halloween is their busiest season.

When they opened the wedding chapel several years ago, there was some opposition from local folks who were concerned about the propriety of using religious symbols on a building in a town called Hell, so Colone had a large metal question mark fashioned that sits atop the chapel's steeple.

Among the many souvenirs that you can purchase in Hell are a bottle of dehydrated water from Hell Creek, a one-inch-square piece of land in Hell, and baseball bats labeled "A bat out of Hell, Michigan." They also have license plate brackets, tee shirts, postcards, and bumper stickers with the town name prominently displayed.

Perhaps the most amusing thing sold is the right to become "mayor for a day" in Hell. For a nominal fee, the day begins with the honoree being awakened early in the morning by a phone call advising him, or her, of the honor and the title that has been bestowed on them. This is followed throughout the day with other phone calls alerting the "mayor" to various imaginary disasters that have just occurred in the tiny community and asking him or her to solve the dilemma. The "mayor" also receives a grab-bag full of souvenirs, a key to the village, and suitable proclamations. The big day ends in the evening when Colone phones the "mayor" and informs them that, with regret, the village has decided to impeach them for not solving all the problems.

I guess you could say this is a "helluva" One Tank Trip.

Hell
4045 Patterson Lake Rd • Hell, MI   734-878-2233
www.gotohellmi.com

Actually, if you get bored in Hell, there are many other things to see and do in the area. See other chapters in this book or contact:

Livingston County Convention & Visitors Bureau
www.lccvb.org • 517-548-1795

Henry Ford's Attic

Michigan: Dearborn

Ford was born in Michigan—both the man and the car. Dearborn is home to the headquarters of the giant Ford Motor Company. But it is probably best known as the home of the **Henry Ford Museum and Greenfield Village**, an institution that many people refer to as "The Nation's Attic" or "Henry's Garage."

Most school kids have probably, sometime in their young lives, made the trek to Dearborn to wander through the huge museum or to walk up and down the streets of another era in Greenfield Village.

Here you will find homes and businesses of people who changed our world. There's the Wright brothers' Bicycle Shop, from Dayton, Ohio; the Menlo Park laboratories of another Ohioan, Thomas Edison; and the farm that once belonged to Harvey Firestone out in Columbiana County, Ohio. All of these are the actual buildings, dozens upon dozens of historic buildings spanning more than 300 years of our history, moved here, brick by brick, board by board, by order of auto magnate Henry Ford, starting nearly 90 years ago, when he began constructing Dearborn, and Michigan's, greatest attraction.

The enclosed 88-acre site is like some giant time machine. Even the maintenance workers in Greenfield Village do not travel in modern vehicles. You are likely to see them either riding antique bicycles or tooling around in trucks that were made nearly a century ago. Costumed interpreters at many of the homes and businesses add to the illusion that somehow you have entered a time warp and are back at the beginning of America's adventure.

Visitors can take a paddlewheel boat ride around a lagoon, ride a steam train around the perimeter of the village, or travel in a horse-drawn omnibus. They can watch sheep being herded on the village green, peek into Henry Ford's first garage, where he invented his first automobile. And that is just for openers. There are a host of homes and businesses that affected all of our lives and are now located here.

Next door is the giant Henry Ford Museum, which previous visitors will be happy to learn has now been air conditioned, making summer

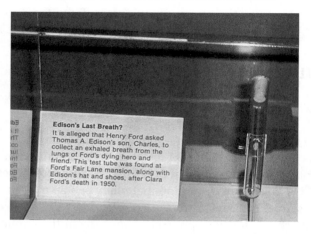

Edison's Last Breath?

It is alleged that Henry Ford asked Thomas A. Edison's son, Charles, to collect an exhaled breath from the lungs of Ford's dying hero and friend. This test tube was found at Ford's Fair Lane mansion, along with Edison's hat and shoes, after Clara Ford's death in 1950.

The glass vial that purportedly contains the last earthly breath of Thomas Edison.

visits far more comfortable. You can find everything from giant loco-motives to one of the finest collections of automobiles in the world.

One of my favorite exhibits is a glass vial that says it contains the "last earthly breath of Thomas A. Edison." But historians at the museum express some doubt over the exhibit. Near the vial is a lengthy story of how the test tube came to be associated with Edison's last hour on Earth. Whether Charles Edison, Thomas Edison's son, who was in the room at the time he died in 1931, actually captured his father's last breath or just capped an open test tube that was in the room, is open to speculation. What we do know is that he gave the test tube to Henry Ford, and that is what you see today.

There are everyday things on display, such as a table radio from the 1920s, as well as an exact, full-size replica of Lindbergh's *Spirit of St. Louis* airplane, in which he flew across the Atlantic Ocean. There are even full-size buildings, such as a diner from the 1940s, a giant Holiday Inn sign from the 1950s, and other things associated with travel.

One of the more unusual exhibits is R. Buckminster Fuller's Dymax-ion House. It's the only surviving prototype of the round, aluminum homes that Fuller hoped would be the answer to cheap, affordable housing after World War II. The home had a circular floor plan, with cupboards and drawers that disappear into the walls, and a window plan that gave the owners a panoramic view of their neighborhood. It also had a bathroom that you just have to see. It defies description.

The last surviving Dymaxion House, designed by R. Buckminster Fuller.

The round, aluminum home idea just never caught on, and this model is the last known one in existence.

They also have an exhibit of presidential limousines, including the iconic Lincoln convertible that John F. Kennedy was riding in on the day he was assassinated in Dallas, Texas.

The Henry Ford is more than a museum. It truly is a family experience, and one of my long-time-favorite One Tank Trips.

Just across the parking lot is another museum.

The **Automotive Hall of Fame** claims to be the only industry-wide institution to honor the men and women responsible for the invention and creation of automobiles. It combines names of the great auto pioneers, including Ford, the Fisher brothers, the Dodge brothers, and probably more than a few names you have never heard of, with some classic cars and museum exhibits that trace both the history of car making and the development of the American highway system.

One caution: If you are planning to visit the hall of fame, I would do this before heading for the Ford Museum and Greenfield Village. While the exhibits at the Automotive Hall of Fame are interesting, and, I am sure, of great importance to the folks in the auto industry, they pale in comparison to the massive size and number of exhibits next door at Greenfield Village and the Ford Museum.

And, before you leave, there's one final thing to see.

Built prior to World War I, the giant River Rouge complex was Henry Ford's dream of building a factory where raw materials would flow into one end of the structure and a finished, manufactured product would roll off the assembly line at the other end. In its prime, the plant was a complex of 93 buildings that stretched a mile and a half wide by a mile long and employed 100,000 workers! Many famous Ford products were born here, including the popular Mustang automobile.

Today, the renovated, down-sized plant encompasses about 600 acres and the workforce has shrunken to a few thousand workers, but it is still Ford's largest manufacturing facility.

You can tour the facility and visit the final assembly plant for Ford F-150 trucks. You must get tickets for the tour at the Henry Ford Museum, and a bus takes you to the plant's visitors center (you are not allowed to drive to the plant).

A virtual theater lets you experience the sights, sounds, and even the feel of what it is like to build an automobile. When the audience is surrounded by video of blast furnaces roaring, you feel the heat. When cars go through a paint booth on the screen, the audience feels a warm mist enveloping them. (It's only water.) And the final scene of sitting behind the wheel of a newly made car can be almost as thrilling as driving a real vehicle.

Another attraction is the opportunity to go to the observation deck and look down on the 10-acre plant roof covered with grass to help make the plant cooler in summer and warmer in winter. It's said to be the largest rooftop garden in the world.

The other observation deck over the assembly line allows you to see the last stages of construction of Ford trucks.

You also get to see a cavalcade of the cars and trucks that were once built here, including the original Mustang.

That's a lot to see and do in just one location.

The Henry Ford
20900 Oakwood Blvd • Dearborn, MI   313-982-6001
www.thehenryford.org

Automotive Hall of Fame
21400 Oakwood Blvd • Dearborn, MI   313-240-4000
www.automotivehalloffame.org

The Ultimate Driving Experience

Indiana: Indianapolis

Some years ago, we did a week-long series of One Tank Trips to Indiana. My favorite memory from that trip was a visit to a race-driving school in Indianapolis that lets amateurs like me get behind the wheel of a real race car.

Bear in mind that I have never been known to race even my family car, let alone one of the super-powered race cars that call Indianapolis home.

We were set up with a firm called Fast Company that offered, for a fee, a "race driver experience."

All I had to do was sit through a morning-long course in driving and safety before I would get the chance to actually strap myself into a real racing car and go throttle-to-the-wall around the great oval track.

I must admit that, while I thought my reflexes were, at that time, pretty good, I had never considered what it was like out on a track.

The instructor droned on and on about the speed needed to take the curves, braking at key points on the track, the science of racing, and—the part that really got my attention—what to do if I lost control and hit the wall. He basically said the car was made to absorb much of the collision, but he added a little prayer wouldn't be a bad idea at such a time.

Finally, the class ended and three of us, all novices, were taken to the side of the racetrack, where we were outfitted with a full helmet and neck brace and a pair of flame-retardant driving gloves, and introduced to our cars.

They were small, sleek, Renault open-cockpit, single-seat race cars capable of speeds up to about 200 mph!

We were strapped into the cars and, one at a time, we joined a line behind a souped-up pickup truck that would lead us around the track for a couple of laps. Then we would have a three-lap race.

The roar of the engine could be heard through the helmet, even at a relatively slow speed, as we circled the track like a trio of baby ducks following the much larger pick-up truck.

When the instructor was satisfied that we knew how to work the

Though neck-and-neck as we flashed by the camera, I finished in second place. The winner's top speed was 130 mph; mine was 92 mph. *(Fox8 TV)*

accelerator and the brakes and had managed to circle the track a couple of times without running into each other, he signaled us to a stop and said the race was on.

We took one lap side by side, and as we approached the starting line, a man with a flag watched us carefully as we drew closer and closer. Then he suddenly waved the flag up and down, and we were off.

I just remember seeing the flagman flash by out of the corner of my eye as I floored the accelerator and gripped the steering wheel so tightly I'm amazed it didn't bend.

The roar of the motor was much louder now. As I approached the first curve, I had to fight the instinct to stomp on the brakes. I did let off the accelerator and paid for it as one of my opponents went roaring by me.

The laps went fairly quickly. I dared not even look at the control panel. Empty spectator stands flashed by like a picket fence. I guessed that I might be traveling at 150 miles per hour or better.

I saw one of my opponents cross the finish line well ahead of me. I tried to look around to see where the third car was as I also roared by the finish line.

It turned out that I had come in second. The winner's top speed was 130 mph. My speed: 92 mph. The third person in the race was apparently intimidated by the speed of the winning car, and he dropped so far back that his top speed never got over 75 mph. Mario Andretti has nothing to fear from the three of us.

It was an experience that I have always remembered. I had hoped to update the trip for this book with current information about the racing company that I used that day, but I was unable to find them.

However, there are similar operations in the Indianapolis area.

The one that was recommended to me by the local tourism and convention bureau was **Indy Racing Experience**, which offers you the chance to actually drive a car that has competed in the Indianapolis 500 race.

They also offer several options for those who want to ride along, rather than drive.

If you are looking for that once-in-a-lifetime experience, this might be just the thing.

Indy Racing Experience
2A Gasoline Alley • Indianapolis, IN   888-357-5002
www.indyracingexperience.com

If you are looking for places to stay and other things to do, contact:

Visit Indy
www.visitindy.com • 317-262-3000

Indiana's Giant Flea

Indiana: Shipshewana

Some folks may dispute it, but Hoosiers say that this is the biggest flea market in the Midwest.

It is a claim that is hard to dispute. The **Shipshewana Auction & Flea Market** is located in the town of Shipshewana, over the Ohio line in Indiana, and covers 100 acres. On a good day, they have more than 900 vendors set up in neat rows and an auction barn with more than a half–dozen auctioneers all chanting at the same time, making it sound like the biblical Tower of Babel.

Tour buses from surrounding states fill the parking lots each Tuesday and Wednesday.

In the barn, you can find everything on the auction block from a wooden cigar store Indian to a broken-down 1930s Maytag washing machine.

The auction started in 1922, and the flea market followed a couple of years later. It has continued to grow over the years, and today attracts an estimated half-million visitors to the small town each year. Depending on the time of year, the auction barn has seven to 10 auctioneers selling different items, their chants competing with each other as they attempt to sell off the week's accumulation of items that have been brought to the barn. The auction starts at 9:00 a.m. on Wednesdays and runs until mid-afternoon when the barn is sold out.

On Tuesdays and Wednesdays, on the grounds of the surrounding flea market, you will find everything from fresh vegetables and fruit to tube socks and bird houses. There are stands that sell things you probably didn't even know that you needed, as well as stands run by everyday folks who are trying to make a few dollars by cleaning out the attic or garage and becoming flea market merchants for a day.

The place has the air of a carnival come to town. In fact, one of the permanent exhibitors in the middle of the flea market could easily qualify for a summertime carnival. It's "Poor Ol' George's Fun Spot." They don't sell anything. They advertise their displays as just "weird stuff to look at," and they charge a buck to enter and gawk at it. The "stuff" includes a model of a small Amish buggy pulled by a pig, a

Hoosiers claim this is the biggest flea market in the Midwest.

life-size "throne" owner George Borum built for Elvis, or you can have your picture taken with a life-size photo of the world's tallest man. Borum is a well-known regional folk artist who tries to put a country spin on the Fun Spot by misspelling words and even advertises it as a "First Klass Tourist Trap."

Perhaps the best way to see the flea market is to pick up the free official visitors' guide that tells you where to find everything from spices to underwear. It also provides a map of downtown Shipshewana and the surrounding area and lists of all the various inns and motels where you can stay while visiting the town.

Shipshewana is a tiny farming community in the northeastern corner of Indiana. It was named for Chief Shipshewana of the Potawatomi tribe who once lived there. There is also a heavy influence of the "plain people" of the Amish and Mennonite religions. Bearded men and bonneted women in horse-drawn carriages are a common sight in the town. Neat gardens line the well-kept streets and most businesses are closed on Sunday in accordance with Amish and Mennonite beliefs. It is said that this area of Indiana is the third-largest population of Amish in the world. (The first and second largest are Ohio and Pennsylvania, respectively.)

If you would like to learn more about the Amish life, you can visit Menno-Hof, the Mennonite and Amish Heritage Center, not far from the flea market. The complex offers hands-on exhibits as it tells the story of 500 years of their history. You can also get an up-close look at the everyday life of the Amish, who still live with coal oil lamps, farm with horses, and use buggies for transportation. One of the highlights of the tour is the interactive "Tornado Theater," where the audience can feel the wind blow and the room shake as a movie of a tornado bearing down on the Midwest is shown.

The town also offers a variety of small shops that sell antiques, farming supplies, and fabrics. There is a plentiful supply of bed-and-breakfast inns and some motels nearby. For the kids, there are several parks with small lakes and beaches. Shipshewana can be a great family trip.

Shipshewana Auction & Flea Market
345 S Van Buren St (State Route 5) • Shipshewana, IN   260-768-4129
www.tradingplaceamerica.com

The local merchants' association has a website that offers lots of ideas for places to stay and things to see and do:

Shipshewana Retail Merchants Association
www.shipshewana.com • 260-768-7589

Where Ducks Walk on the Fish

Pymatuning Lake straddles the Ohio-Pennsylvania border in Ashtabula County in northeastern Ohio. It is one of my favorite One Tank Trips because it is home to the place where the ducks walk on the backs of the fish.

The **Linesville Spillway**, on the Pennsylvania side of the lake, has become the gathering place for probably hundreds of thousands of two- and even three-foot-long carp. Feeding the fish is a favorite tourist activity: When a piece of day-old bread is tossed into the water, the surface of the lake explodes into a roiling cauldron of hungry fish.

Signs abound with roadside merchants selling loaves of stale bread to tourists to use as fish food. In fact, so much bread has been fed to the fish over the years that environmentalists are now concerned that it might affect the eco-balance of the lake.

At the recently remodeled and enlarged visitor area at the spillway, tossing a slice of moldy bread onto the waters causes an eruption as thousands of hungry carp, their snouts madly poking out of the water, lunge for the bread. They also compete with wild ducks and geese that literally walk on top of the churning fish to get a beak full of the soggy dough. The huge, bubbling mass of fish reminds onlookers of the fabled piranhas of the Amazon River and how quickly they attack, devouring anything unfortunate enough to have fallen into the river.

I once asked the operator of the concession stand whether anyone had ever fallen into the water while feeding the carp. He admitted that he had recently taken a tumble himself while cleaning up debris along the water's edge.

"What happened?" I asked.

He replied that he had scrambled back out of the water so quickly that the fish hardly knew he was there. He said he believed that although the fish might nibble at a human, he didn't think they would actually bite or harm a person. But, he added, he didn't want to stay in the water long enough to test his theory.

The name "Pymatuning" comes from early Native Americans who once inhabited the area, and translates to "the crooked-mouthed

Millions of hungry carp fight for bread tossed into the water by tourists. The fish compete with wild ducks for the treat.

man's dwelling place." Legend has it that the name didn't refer to a facial disfigurement but more to the man's ability to tell lies.

Fourteen thousand years ago, as the great glacier that covered much of the North American continent started to melt, it left in its wake "kettle" lakes: small depressions dug out by the glacial movement and filled with melting glacier ice that eventually grew into great swamps in the rolling countryside. Two rivers in Pennsylvania also were formed by the glacier's retreat: the Shenango and the Beaver Rivers that flowed into the marshy swamp area.

In 1933, during the Great Depression, a flood control dam was built to manage the flow of the rivers. It created the reservoir of water that became Pymatuning Lake.

Today, the lake sprawls across 14,000 acres on both sides of the Ohio-Pennsylvania border, and has become one of the top recreational areas in both states. It's considered one of the best fishing spots in Ohio. Walleye is the prize catch, but there are also catfish, crappie, bluegill, and bass. And, oh yes, let's not forget the carp.

Linesville Spillway
2 miles south of Linesville on the Hartstown Rd • Linesville, PA
724-932-3141

For more things to see and do in the area, contact:

Crawford County Convention and Visitors Bureau
www.visitcrawford.org • 814-333-1258

A Train Trip to Titusville

Pennsylvania: Titusville

The western edge of Pennsylvania abutting Ohio has some of the most scenic, rolling, historic countryside in the country and makes for enjoyable One Tank Trips, especially in late summer.

Titusville, Pennsylvania, has always been one of my favorite destinations in the Keystone State because I like trains.

The **Oil Creek and Titusville Railroad** doesn't really go very far, just about 14 miles. But, in those miles, you travel through the place where the modern-day oil industry was born.

It was in Titusville in 1859 that Col. Edwin Drake drilled the first commercial oil well. You can still see a replica of that original well in the Drake State Park.

You will see more than oil wells on your train ride. You cross scenic rivers and often spot wildlife such as eagles, turkeys, and even black bear.

The Oil Creek and Titusville Railroad has another distinction. It is the only train still running in the United States that has an official operating U.S. Mail car. Mail cars, where the mail was sorted and delivered as the train traveled from one city to another, started in 1863

The Oil Creek and Titusville Railroad tourist train, making a run through Drake Park where the oil industry in the U.S. began.

during the Civil War. At railroads' peak in the twentieth century, there were 9,000 train routes covering nearly a quarter of a million miles in North America. With the increasing use of airlines to carry mail, the last railroad mail route closed in June 1977.

Ten years later, when the Oil Creek and Titusville Railroad began operation, they convinced the U.S. Postal Service to let them use an historic mail car as a traveling post office. You can mail a postcard or letter aboard the train, and it will have a one-of-a-kind railway postage cancellation mark.

One more reason to visit Titusville is a unique motel where you can spend the night.

The Caboose Motel, owned by the Oil Creek and Titusville Railroad, is made up of 21 real railroad cabooses, each painted in the colors of one of the railroad lines that once crossed America. Each of the motel "rooms" is modern, with air-conditioning, a full bath, TV and even Wi-Fi.

Oil Creek and Titusville Railroad
409 Perry St • Titusville, PA   814-827-6228
www.octrr.org

Seven Miles of Beaches

Pennsylvania: Erie

When someone asks me about my favorite beach on the shore of Lake Erie, I point them towards Pennsylvania.

Presque Isle State Park is unique for many reasons. First and foremost, it is a peninsula that runs seven miles into Lake Erie. It also offers sandy beaches that stretch for miles and encourage kite flying, volleyball, and family swimming. There are sand dunes and places to watch world-class sunsets.

Presque Isle is not an island, despite its name, which is French for "almost island," and it played an important role in U.S. history.

During the War of 1812, Commodore Oliver Hazard Perry constructed six of the nine ships in his fleet at Presque Isle Bay. After the Battle of Lake Erie, which Perry won, he returned to Presque Isle's Misery Bay near the peninsula, where his men spent the winters through 1814. The place was named Misery Bay because of the hardships that Perry's sailors faced when smallpox broke out. Many of

My favorite beach on Lake Erie is at Presque Isle State Park. *(Visit Erie)*

those who died were buried in what is now called Graveyard Pond in the park.

Today, the peninsula is a recreational oasis covering more than 3,200 acres that looks across the bay to Erie, the fourth-largest city in Pennsylvania.

The entire peninsula is now a state park, and you can drive the 14 miles it takes to circle the park. On the lake side are a number of beaches with parking lots and bath houses.

On the bay side that faces downtown Erie, you will find paved all-purpose trails for walking, running, and biking. There are several small parks for picnicking and parking lots with boat ramps.

As you get near the tip of the peninsula, you will find woods with many deer and wild turkey. There are also marshes, creeks, and streams. This is also the area where you can rent boats and bicycles if you did not bring your own.

Near the Perry Monument, you can take a ride on board the *Lady Kate*, which in another life was a ferry-boat at Cedar Point in Sandusky, Ohio. The *Lady Kate* gives a hour-and-a-half tour of the bay and Lake Erie.

It is a fun way to see and learn more about Presque Isle.

Presque Isle State Park
301 Peninsula Dr • Erie, PA   814-833-7424
www.presqueisle.org

For more about the Erie area, see other chapters in this book or:

Visit Erie
www.visiteriepa.com • 800-524-3743

Some Holiday Traditions Just Across the State Line

Pennsylvania: Hermitage, Sharon

Families from three states have made a holiday tradition of traveling to Sharon, Pennsylvania, to kick off their Christmas celebration.

It all started way back in the early 1960s, when the folks who operate **Kraynak's Garden Center in Hermitage**, a suburb of Sharon, were searching for a way to increase their income during the winter months.

At first it was just some artificial Christmas trees and a few ornaments. But that soon grew into more trees, decorations, and even toys.

But the real beginning was the year someone suggested that a storage room be changed during the holidays to resemble a department store window with decorated trees and animated figures. People crowded the store to see the display.

That single display has now grown to a 300-foot-long hallway display that replicates many department store windows.

As you walk through the winding hallway, you'll see elves, animated deer, skaters, fireplaces, Santa and his sleigh, and hundreds of stuffed and animated animals of every description.

Dan Zippie, grandson of the founder of Kraynak's, told me they start working on the display for the coming year in January. They start decorating trees and building new sets beginning in June, and usually find themselves still working the night before the display, now known as "Christmasland," opens in September.

Christmasland runs daily from September to December 31. Admission is free.

Zippie told me that over the last 50 years, they have had people come from every state in America and all over the world to experience their free display.

"We hope they buy something," he said, "but we also get paid in the smiles on the faces of the children."

Christmasland is located along the side of the building that houses 20,000 square feet of toys and trains. Talk about Santa Claus's Workshop!

"Chocolate Kingdom" at Daffin's Candies. *(Daffin's Candies)*

You enter the store and walk through the toys to enter the Christmasland Display. As you go through the door, you'll hear music above the chatter of excited youngsters strolling down the long hall, peering at hundreds of beautifully decorated trees. Thousands of stuffed and animated figures dance, skate, climb, and fly across fantasy scenes of forests, fields, living rooms with fireplaces, ice palaces, bubbling fountains, and pools.

The displays change every year with the addition of new animation and the refurbishing of some of the early characters that have been used and reused since the 1960s.

Zippie pointed to some skating snowmen and said they seem to be crowd favorites. They appear, with new attire, each year in a different showcase.

The display is a mixture of fantasy and traditional holiday scenes. The last display is always a manger scene with the wise men and baby Jesus.

As you leave the hall of Christmasland, you enter a greenhouse awash with a sea of colorful poinsettias that fills the eye as far as you can see.

From there, you wander through another building filled with Christmas decorations of every size and color.

The final stop brings you back into the giant toy store, where you will find much more than the toys you discover in the big-box stores. They also carry educational and unique toys, even some from regional manufacturers.

In nearby Sharon is another attraction that is a natural fit in the holidays: The world's largest candy store.

At least, that is the claim of **Daffin's Candies**.

The store on State Street is nearly 20,000 square feet, and when you stand at one end of the candy counter, you see every conceivable kind of chocolate and chocolate-covered candy you can imagine stretching almost half the length of a football field.

Connie Leon, the manager, pointed out that what also makes the store unique is the "Chocolate Kingdom," a room filled with castles, a Ferris wheel, giant turtles bigger than a man, and even a full-size reindeer, all made from chocolate.

The factory where all this wonderful chocolate is made is nearby, and you can arrange to take a tour. While you won't see any elves making the candy, you will get a free sample at the conclusion of the tour.

Kraynak's Garden Center
2525 E State St • Hermitage, PA   724-347-4511
www.kraynaks.com

Daffin's Candies
496 E State St • Sharon, PA   724-342-2892
www.daffins.com

For places to stay or dine, plus other local attractions:

Visit Mercer County, PA
www.visitmercercountypa.com • 800-637-2370

Waldameer Amusement Park

When I am asked what my favorite amusement park is, it's a tough question. I have several. Ohio has two major theme-parks: Cedar Point in Sandusky and Kings Island near Cincinnati, and both are world-class parks that any state would be proud to have. But I am drawn to an old-fashioned "mom-and-pop" amusement park with bargain prices. The one I am talking about is family-owned **Waldameer Park** in nearby Erie, Pennsylvania.

Erie is, of course, just a short drive east of Cleveland on I-90.

Waldameer is German for "woods by the sea." The park is located right at the entrance to another great Pennsylvania attraction, Presque Isle State Park, a peninsula that juts seven miles into Lake Erie.

Let me tell you about Waldameer Amusement Park.

It has been around for almost 120 years. It originally was one of the many "trolley parks"—amusement and picnic areas that could be reached from a nearby community by trolley.

Once there were hundreds of such parks across America. Now, Waldameer is the tenth oldest amusement park still in operation in the nation.

The park is compact and beautifully landscaped. It is located right next to Water World, a water park that the amusement park also operates.

At present, they have more than 75 rides, including four roller coasters.

My personal favorite is the relatively new steel and wood roller coaster, Ravine Flyer II, that stretches more than 3,000 feet and has two thrilling, high-speed, 90-degree banks. It is perhaps the only roller coaster in America that shoots its riders across an arched bridge over a busy four-lane state highway and back in just seconds!

When it became operational in 2008, an amusement park trade group honored the coaster as the best new ride in the world.

Ravine Flyer II has also been rated as one of the top 10 roller coasters in the world by Coaster Grotto, a coaster-enthusiast group that ranks coasters around the globe.

The Ravine Flyer II at Waldameer Amusement Park passes over a four-lane state highway.

This is the second roller coaster at the park to bear the name "Ravine Flyer." The original coaster was involved in a tragedy in 1938 after a mechanical failure stopped the coaster between dips and a passenger carelessly got out of the car and fell to his death. The owner of the park at that time was so distraught that he closed down and dismantled the roller coaster. It was after World War II before another coaster, "The Comet," was built at the park. The best news about Waldameer is parking is free! So is admission to the amusement park. You pay only for the attractions you ride. Most stage shows also are free. And, get this, they encourage you to bring along a picnic basket. They have picnic shelters.

Paul Nelson, the long-time owner of Waldameer told me, "I believe that too many business people are just too damn greedy. We share our wealth with our community."

Nelson has been associated with Waldameer since 1945, when he was 11 years old and got a summer job cleaning bathrooms at the park.

Among the other thrill rides is the Mega Vortex, which is a bit hard to describe. It's a large, revolving disk that goes up and down and back and forth on a 120-foot-long "U" shaped track. Riders sit on motor-cycle-like seats on the edge of the disk as they rotate rapidly up to 50 feet in the air. Another is the "X-Scream," a 140-foot-tall drop tower ride that lets you make a screaming free fall.

Water World does charge admission. It has 16 slides and many other water-themed attractions as well as what they claim is the "Tri-States' largest wave pool."

Waldameer & Water World
220 Peninsula Dr • Erie, PA   814-838-3591
www.waldameer.com

For more ideas in the area, see other chapters in this book or:

VisitErie
www.visiteriepa.com • 800-524-3743

West Virginia State Pen

West Virginia: Moundsville

I have never understood the fascination that law-abiding citizens have with tours of former prisons and jails. But if you are going to visit one, you might as well tour what was once described by the U.S. Justice Department as one of the top 10 "most violent correctional facilities" in America.

The old **West Virginia State Penitentiary** was modeled on Joliet Prison in Illinois. Land for the prison was purchased in 1866 in Moundsville, selected because it was only a few miles from Wheeling, which at the time was the state capital.

The castle-like structure was built so that the appearance would give to incoming inmates "a cheerless blank, indicative of the misery that awaits the unhappy being who enters within its walls."

Criminals, both famous and infamous, were held here, including Eugene V. Debs, who was accused of espionage in World War I. He ran for president as a socialist candidate five times.

While serving time in a California prison, mass killer Charles Manson wrote to the governor of West Virginia in 1983 asking to be

West Virginia Penitentiary at Moundsville. *(Pghjared, CC BY 2.0 , goo.gl/p54unu)*

transferred to the Moundsville prison because he was a native of the state. He was refused.

Because it was a state prison and held the worst of the worst, 94 men were executed here for their crimes. From 1899 to 1949, hanging was the preferred method of execution. On the public tour, guides will show you where the gallows were and how they worked. Until June 19, 1931, the public could attend executions. However, on that date, a man who was being put to death for the murder of his wife was so heavy that when the trap door was sprung and his full weight hit the rope, the prisoner was instantly decapitated. After that, the state decided that pubic attendance at executions would be by invitation only.

In 1951, the prison switched to electrocution. Nine men died in the electric chair, nicknamed "Old Sparky." It was taken out of commission in 1965 when the West Virginia legislature struck down the death penalty. Today, Old Sparky also can be seen in a tour of the former prison.

The century-old prison was finally closed in the mid-1990s because of its age as well as federal laws concerning prisons and the treatment of prisoners. A local foundation now leases the prison, and it is used for public tours.

The old prison has been featured in at least three Hollywood movies and several national television shows.

West Virginia Penitentiary Tours
818 Jefferson Ave • Moundsville, WV   304-843-6200
www.wvpentours.com

If you are spending the night in the area or looking for other things to do locally, contact:

Greater Moundsville Convention & Visitors Bureau
304-810-4435
www.visitmoundsville.com

AFTERWORDS

Always Check the Date

No matter how busy your life is, you should always keep a calendar. I don't, but my wife Bonnie is usually very good about keeping track of our appointments, and I have grown to rely on her calendar.

Such was the case when, on a Sunday night some years ago, Bonnie reminded me that the very next day, a Monday, I had a speech scheduled for the Packard Music Hall in Warren. When I schedule these things, I give little thought to what weather I might face several months later. It just so happened that this was January and it was snowing, and the forecast did not offer any chance of the snow letting up.

I pride myself on having never missed a speech or personal appearance because of ill health or bad weather. The speech was set for 9:00 a.m., so I set the alarm for 5:00 a.m. to allow myself plenty of time to drive across snow-covered northern Ohio.

The ride from Bay Village to Warren that morning was memorable. The snow had continued to fall throughout the night, and was still coming down as I drove. The wind was whipping the snow, causing whiteouts. It was a white-knuckle drive every mile of the way. Many times during the trip, I thought of giving up and returning home. I anxiously watched the minutes tick by as I struggled to keep my car on the road. Would I make it in time?

Finally, at 8:50 a.m., I spotted the shape of the music hall ahead of me on the right. I slid into the driveway to the parking lot, only to find it empty. The tracks I was leaving in the new fallen snow were the only ones in the parking lot. Mine was the only car. I drove up to a set of double doors. They were locked. Through a window I saw only darkness.

I grabbed my cell phone and called Kevin Salyer in Cleveland, who set up my personal appearances. "Kevin," I nearly shouted, "I have just driven through a snowstorm to Warren to the Packard Music Hall to give a speech, and not only is no one here, but the building is locked up."

Kevin told me to calm down and get out my copy of the letter inviting me. I did. He said to re-read the date and time. I did. It said I was invited on January 19th. This was January 19th. It said the meeting was to start at 9:00 a.m. The time was exactly 9:00 a.m.!

"Read the rest of it." Kevin urged.

I did.

I was one year early for the speech.

On the Bookselling Trail

If you write a book, sooner or later you will be invited to speak at an event and promote it. Probably every author has experienced at least one event that makes him or her wonder what the event planner was thinking.

I had just such an experience.

In fairness to the community and the well-meaning committee person who suggested I be invited, I won't name the town. Let's just say it was in north central Ohio.

The event was held in the local school. It was a hot summer night, and the school was not air conditioned. Oh, yes, they also neglected to tell me that it was not only "family night," but also "bring your family pet night."

I arrived about 10 minutes before I was to speak, and was met by the committee chairman and escorted into a side door to the gymnasium. A blast of humid air hit me in the face as I entered the door. The humidity was accompanied by the roar of a giant fan, on loan from the local fire department, which made a feeble attempt to lower the jungle-like heat of the gym. All of this was joined by the raucous sound of a number of children of all ages who were screaming, laughing, and chasing each other up and down the aisles while parents used newspapers and pieces of boxes as makeshift fans.

Then the committee person, still smiling, led me to a microphone. When he turned on the microphone, there was a loud squeal and an enormous popping sound from the amplifier, which promptly started smoking. While other members of the committee quickly unplugged the now-fried electronics, the head of the committee said, "Sorry, you will have to just talk a bit louder." So, there I stood, sweat dripping off the end of my nose, shouting to be heard over the roar of the giant fan and the noise of restless children. I really couldn't imagine the whole situation getting any worse.

I was wrong.

Did I mention it was "Bring your family pet" night?

I had been talking, or rather, shouting, for about five minutes when an English sheepdog got into a dispute with a Great Dane. The dogs went at each other just below the lip of the stage where I stood. I had to pause while anxious owners of the dogs tried to separate them.

Then, believe it or not, a chicken walked out onto the stage and started to peck at my shoes. Again, I had to stop my presentation while the young person who owned the chicken ran out onto the stage, to the hilarity of the audience, to scoop up his pet.

Somehow, I staggered through the presentation, reminding myself that this is what you have to do to sell books.

The committee had asked me to afterward sit at a table, chat with members of the audience, and sign copies of my books. I had just sat down when I sensed someone behind me who suddenly draped a rather large thing around my neck and shoulders.

Did I mention that I have a real fear of snakes?

The chairman of the committee, thinking it would make a great photo opportunity for the crowd, had borrowed someone's six-foot-long boa constrictor and had placed it around my neck and shoulders, where it immediately began to tighten-its coils.

No animals were injured that evening, but I think my screams and curses probably frightened several dogs and children as I pleaded, no, demanded in language not meant for a PTA meeting that somebody get the snake off me.

Another time, I was invited to speak at a local library in a room meant to hold about 175 people. More than 200 showed up. There were so many people that the librarians had to move the podium back almost to the wall, and I had rows of people sitting directly in front of me. They were so close, I could have reached out and touched them.

As I closed my talk, I picked up a glass of ice water on the podium and turned to edge my way out of the room, when my feet got tangled up in some wires leading to the public address system on the floor. As I went down, the glass of ice-water went flying into the air, soaking people in the first, second, and third rows. In falling, I also took down the public address system, yanking the microphone off the podium and the speakers off the walls where they were mounted. The fall knocked the wind out of me, and as I was lying there on my back, I had my eyes closed, mentally taking stock of what did and did not hurt.

I opened my eyes and saw a young blonde girl with huge horn-rimmed glasses just inches away from my face.

"Can I help you?" she shouted. "I'm a Girl Scout, and I can get a merit badge if I do. Please let me help you."

I don't know whether she got the merit badge. I survived with only a couple of bruises. I probably lost a few customers, those too soaked to stick around and buy a book.

When you are promoting a book, especially a book about travel, you sometimes have to think outside the box. Some years ago, when my first book was published, I decided that it would be helpful when speaking to large audiences if I could also show them pictures of what I was talking about.

Now, bear in mind that this was still in the era before cell phones, iPads, video projectors, and most electronic gadgets that we take for granted today. What we did have was a device called the carousel projector, made by Kodak, that projected 35mm color slides onto a screen or large wall. It was called a carousel because the round tray on top that contained up to 100 slides rotated, dropping a fresh color slide in front of the projection bulb each time you pressed the remote control button. It was a complicated procedure, and mechanical: As one slide dropped down, another piece of machinery would grab the slide just seen and shoot it back up into the carousel. But it was the world standard for showing pictures to groups at that time. What could possibly go wrong?

I had been invited to speak about my book to an antique car club in Sandusky. They were holding their meeting in the ballroom of a local hotel. After I accepted, the organizer suggested that since I was coming to Sandusky to speak to their group, perhaps I might come early, say at noon, to take part in their cruise around Sandusky Bay towns and villages in their classic cars. That sounded like fun, and besides, again, what could possibly go wrong?

It turned out, just about everything.

For openers, this was early November and although we had had a series of beautiful autumn days, the day of my speech dawned to the sound of sleet and rain on the roof. I was sure they would cancel the road tour. I was wrong.

I was seated in the back seat of a 1935 Ford Convertible. Did I say back seat? I meant the rumble seat. A rumble seat was a seat that pulled out from where the trunk of the car would be. The convertible top covered the front seat, but not the rumble seat. As we wheeled down the road, it was cold. Then the sleet changed to snow flurries.

The club members took pity on me, pulled over, and found a 1933 four-door Essex automobile for me to ride in. This car had a roof and windows, but no heater. With three of us in the car—the owner, his wife, and me—the windows began to fog over. After we nearly had an accident, they decided to put me into yet another car. This time it was a 1953 Packard. It had not only windows and a roof, but a good heater as well.

However, when we all left Castalia to return to Sandusky, the Packard I was in was the last car to leave the parking lot. As we traveled down a country road, the motor started misfiring, and we fell farther and farther behind the rest of the classic automobiles. Finally, the motor just stopped, and we coasted onto the berm of the road. No matter how many times the owner tried to restart the car, it failed. Finally, with the starter sounding weaker and weaker, he gave up. Did I mention this was back before cell phones? So, there we were, stuck on the side of the road, miles from a town or a telephone.

The owner of the Packard was able to flag down a passing motorist who had room for just one person in his vehicle, and it was agreed I would stay behind to wait while the owner went to find help. He didn't return until almost two hours later. The temperature outside and inside of the car had dropped to the low 40s, and I was tired, cold, and hungry.

We finally got back to the hotel as the dinner was wrapping up and just in time for my speech. I was not in a very good mood as I quickly set up my slide projector and ran the long cord from the projector to the podium. I also had not eaten since early morning, and I was still wearing the damp clothes from the afternoon joy ride in the sleet and snow storm, but I was there to sell books, so I sucked it up and began my speech.

I pressed the remote to bring up the first color slide. That worked fine, but when I attempted to change the slide, the carousel jammed. I stopped my talk, excused myself, ran from the podium to where the projector was set up, and attempted to clear the jam. I thought I had succeeded, and returned to the stage.

Moving swiftly along to the next story that required a photograph, I hit the remote button. There was a "twang!" from the projector, which suddenly started shooting slides 10 or 15 feet into the air. The crowd started laughing as slides rained down on them.

That was the last time I included a slide presentation with my talks.

To make the day complete, when I finally left the hotel to get my car to go home, I discovered I had a flat tire.

The perfect ending to a memorable day.

My Appreciation

I want to thank some people who have been involved in my life and One Tank Trips down through the years.

While it would take another book to list everyone, the following folks have played a large part in the creation and the support of this book.

First, my publisher, David Gray of Gray & Company. David and I first met back in the mid-1990s when I had written my first book. David is a brilliant young man and is a joy to work with.

Chris Andrikanich, who as marketing director for Gray & Co. did so much more than handle marketing. He set up my speeches and personal appearances. He corrected my mistakes and lack of ability in social media. He is a kind and gentle man with a wealth of tech knowledge.

Rob Lucas served for many years as editor of some of my previous books. If you look up patience in the dictionary, Rob's picture should be there. A multi-talented young man who understands our new media world and is gaining worldwide attention for his movie about Cleveland sport star Stella Walsh.

Kevin Salyer, vice-president of programming at Fox 8 TV. I have known Kevin since he started as a young college student many years ago in the promotion department at Fox 8. It was Kevin who brought me back to television in 2012 after I had retired from TV in 2004.

Tomi Toyama-Ambrose, producer of New Day Cleveland on Fox 8 TV whom I jokingly refer to as my "work-daughter." Tomi and I have been friends since she began working at Fox 8 in the 1990's. I have had the pleasure of working with her as producer and director of my One Tank Trips segments since returning to Fox 8 in 2012. We shared many adventures over the years.

Herb Thomas, Fox 8 videographer. Herb and I have worked together for well over 40 years and Herb was the prime videographer who traveled with me and shot the majority of the travel segments we did since 2012.

Kathy Smith, video editor at Fox 8 TV. A veteran editor, Kathy and I have also worked together for over thirty years and she has been responsible for the on-air appearance of a majority of my One Tank Trips over the years.

Craig Zurcher, my son, who started out tagging along on my trips when he was only four years old and ended up spending his summers through high school appearing with me on the show, has now gone full circle and has become videographer and editor of my blog, www.onetanktrips.com.

My wife, Bonnie, who travels with me and shares the driving these days as we explore Ohio and other states looking for new One Tank Trips.

This is the most dangerous part, because I am certain to overlook or forget some person and I shall feel very bad when I discover I neglected to thank them. But here it goes.

There are a wealth of people that I turn to for advice and they include my daughter Melody McCallister, her husband, Ernie McCallister, my daughter, Melissa Luttmann, her husband, Peter Luttmann, my grandchildren, Allison McCallister, Bryan McCallister, Ryan Luttmann and Jason Luttmann. Also there is: Kevin Ruic, Bruce Hamilton, Dan Coughlin, Terry Trakas, Nancy and Dick Rossi, Tom and Fran Currier, Richard and Barb Harris, Ruth and Clyde Harris, my brother and sister-in-law, Noel and Linda Zurcher, Rebecca Brandau, David Glime, Rob Currier, Don Currier, Mary Jo Harris, Trish Bates.

A big thank you also goes to all the folks who have worked with me over the last forty years at Fox 8. The videographers who shared my trips, the editors who made the pieces come alive, the management who gave me the freedom to roam where I pleased and most of all, you, the reader and viewers who made it all possible.

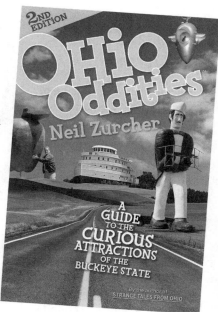

More tales from Neil Zurcher . . .

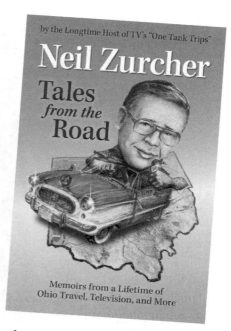

by the Longtime Host of TV's "One Tank Trips"

Neil Zurcher
Tales *from the* Road

Memoirs from a Lifetime of Ohio Travel, Television, and More

After a million miles and four decades as a TV reporter, Neil Zurcher has a lot of great stories to tell . . .

He met Prince Charles in a bathroom, and tripped and fell on President Gerald Ford.

He raced on an elephant, piloted a glider, and hung from a trapeze.

He survived a hotel fire and a tornado. He was tear-gassed at an anti-war protest and almost trapped inside the Ohio Penitentiary during a riot. He drove in a day-long high-speed police chase from Cleveland to Kentucky, and got lost in the middle of Lake Erie.

He rode in jet boats, jet fighters, sternwheelers, a World War II tank, and almost every other kind of vehicle imaginable.

He was ordained as a minister in the Free Spirit Association Church and even officiated at a few weddings. And he would do almost anything and go almost anywhere for a good story. In the process he became one of the most popular personalities on Cleveland TV.

This book shares dozens of Neil'is favorite stories. It's a snapshot of Cleveland television in its golden age.

TALES FROM THE ROAD by Neil Zurcher
Paperback / 296 pages / 48 photos

AVAILABLE AT BOOKSTORES
FOR MORE INFO VISIT **WWW.GRAYCO.COM**

Stay connected with Neil . . .
For more One Tank Trips and other
updates check out:

www.OneTankTrips.com